Open anywhere and pick a
Word for the day!

The first thing Joan said, when Suzy told her the idea was, "That's a stupid idea." Suzy immediately knew she had a winner.

Suzy Prudden and her sister, Joan Meijer, created Itty Bitty Publishing in 2015. With well over 150 book authors to date and 62 Best Sellers, they added Compellation books, Quote books and then Suzy had a silly idea just to sell words that people love. She offered the opportunity to put their word in the Your Amazing Itty Bitty® Book of Words with their definition of the word. Then she added a 60 word bio and photo and the book took off. Wherever she went, Suzy sold words. And here they are.

This is a book you put on your coffee table, leave in the bathroom, or keep on your desk. Use it in any way. Ask a question and see what word shows up when you open the book. Use it to pick a word for the day – just open the book. If you don't like the word – choose another one. It's just a fun book to lighten your day.

Pick up a copy of this fun filled book and discover a new word, or meaning, today!

Your Amazing Itty Bitty® Book of Words

270 Words to Educate and Entertain Your Mind

Itty Bitty® Publishing

Published by Itty Bitty® Publishing
A subsidiary of S & P Productions, Inc.

Copyright © 2019

Printed in the United States of America

Itty Bitty Publishing
311 Main Street, Suite D
El Segundo, CA 90245
(310) 640-8885

ISBN: 978-1-950326-40-2

Dedication

My thanks to Nancy Sardella for being part of the conversation that started it all, my sister, Joan Meijer, for telling me it was a stupid idea (and it was in terms of the amount of work it took to make it happen), Craig Duswalt of Rock Your Life for buying the first Word and Donna Burke for toiling away, being tenacious, putting up with authors who refused to get their information in on time, celebrating when authors did get their information in on time, and continuing to be the backbone of Itty Bitty at the same time. And yes, thanks to all the authors who jumped in and thought it was a very cool Pet Rock idea.

Suzy Prudden

Stop by our Itty Bitty® website Directory to find interesting information from our experts.

www.IttyBittyPublishing.com

Table of Contents

Introduction

Acknowledgement

Words by Letter

Introduction

This book created itself from an idea that occurred in a conversation with a friend at a networking event. I was talking with Nancy Sardella, of WRS, a group I've belonged to off and on since 1993, and I said to her; "I have a one author book series, a 15 author compellation book series, a quote book series, why don't I just sell words? People can put their favorite word in a book with their definition and contact information for $100.00." It seemed simple. I told my sister and business partner, Joan, and she said, "That's a stupid idea." And I knew I had my Pet Rock idea. Four days later, in a mastermind I belong to with Craig Duswalt, I sat in the Hot Seat and talked about my idea. From behind me Craig said, "I'll buy one. It's a good idea." I turned to the group of 35 people and said, "How many of you want to buy words?" And 26 people raised their hands. On my way home that evening I called Joan and said, "You know that stupid idea I had the other day? I just sold 26 words and made $2,600.00." Since then we added a photo and short bio for each author and upped the price to $150.00. We have 270 words in this book and you're all doing the numbers. Yes, we took in a goodly amount of money, but its taken 2 years to put this book together and probably cost more than we took in and yes, we'll do it again.

Ideas come to me a mile a minute. What I want you, the reader to know is, an idea is noting unless you act on it. The Word Book is an "out of the box idea." And I acted on it. The first thing that happened was that I got a "Stop" sign. The next thing that happened was I got a "Go" sign. I didn't know how we were going to do it, I just knew we were going to do it. And thanks to Donna Burke, she got it done. 270 people are now published in a book that will be in thousands of homes. Everyone in this book can use it as a marketing tool for their business. Yes, it will be a Best Seller.

We've already started the next one. If you want a Word contact me at suzy@ittybittypublishing.com.

Acknowledgement

I would like to thank and acknowledge Donna Burke, who worked tirelessly for over a year on this book. She was a steamboat going up the rapids of people's emotions, their constant changes to their information, their frustrations and upsets, she kept her cool (at least on the outside) while she made this book happen. Remember there are close to 300 authors in this book. Truly, I don't think this book would have happened without her. My silly idea was definitely a challenging project which she took on and completed in a steadfast and glorious way. Thank you again, Donna.

~ *Suzy Prudden*

Lord Polonius:

What do you read, my lord?

Hamlet:

Words, words, words.

Hamlet, Act 2, Scene 2
~ *William Shakespeare*

Mike Wolf

Mike Wolf is an expert and authority on passive income. As the founder of Mike Wolf Mastery he helps people achieve the lifestyle of their dreams by helping them create indestructible wealth and abundance through cash flowing real estate and other means.
http://mikewolfmastery.com

Abundance

The blissful state of having enough of everything that you could possibly want or need.

Contact Mike Wolf

http://mikewolfmastery.com

mike@mikewolfmastery.com

Melissa Del Toro Schaffner

Hi! I am Melissa Del Toro Schaffner, Voiceover Artist and lifelong Accountability Expert. I help you engage with your ideal clients by providing a clear, warm, professional and charismatic voice for your radio and TV commercials, social media videos (Instagram, YouTube, Facebook), children's books, e-learning tutorials, employee training systems and audio books.

Accountability

Taking personal responsibility, practicing integrity and having the superpower to blaze your own life path.

Contact Melissa Del Toro Schaffner

Email: melissa@melissadeltoro.com

Website: www.melissadeltoro.com

Facebook: https://www.facebook.com/melissadeltorointernational/

Instagram: https://www.instagram.com/melissadeltoro_voiceover

Mary Helen Conroy

Mary Helen Conroy is a reinvention life coach, professional speaker, and workshop presenter. As a change strategist, her practice works with those in midlife and pre-retirement.

Regardless what she's working on, her goal is to remind those over 50 that life is a daring adventure and they're not done yet!

Adventuring

Life is a daring adventure, and I'm not done yet! Neither are you. Go adventuring.

Contact Mary Helen Conroy

Life's a Daring Adventure
5321 Westport Road, Suite 201
Madison, Wisconsin 53704

608-239-7426

maryhelenconroy@gmail.com

www.lifesadaringadventure.com

Cinda Roffman

Cinda Roffman is a certified hypnotherapist working with clients worldwide and at her offices in Westlake Village and Tarzana, CA. She has helped hundreds manage weight, overcome fears, improve sports performance, reduce test anxiety and increase self-confidence. She wrote The POWER In AFFIRMATIONS, a series of guided journals which help people be, do, and have what they want in life.

Affirmation

Repeated positive statements that help people change their thinking to make desired changes in their behavior.

Contact Cinda Roffman

Cinda Roffman,
Certified Hypnotherapist

cinda@cindaroffman.com

www.cindaroffman.com

818-929-4944

Judy Ann Smith

As a Master Healer in the Arts and Sciences, Judy is dedicated in assisting the transmutation of your creative, powerful, abundant soul to express your purpose and achieve greatness in this, Your Life.

Alchemist

Transformational, creative, magical, transmutation, energy, magik, powerful, abundance, expand, Self Mastery

Contact Judy Ann Smith

Judy A Smith
Health Wavez

949- 413-9425

judy@healthwavez.com

Carol Pilkington

As a Spiritual Advisor, Minister, Speaker and Amazon Best Selling Author specializing in grief and over 25 years training in spirituality, Carol helps those in transition and/or experiencing a loss of some kind whether in the present or something unresolved from the past. She helps clients move beyond grief so they can be more present to the life they are currently living.

Alchemy

Turning lead into gold. This is the nature of the transformational process.

Contact Carol Pilkington

Facebook: www.facebook.com/heartcenteredastrologyandmore

LinkedIn: www.linkedin.com/in/solutionsforyou/

Twitter: www.twitter.com/becauseumatter

Website: www.awareandconscious.com

Telephone: 818-975-0587

Lydia Sugarman

Lydia Sugarman has mounted art exhibitions in New York and Moscow, produced Vin Diesel's first short film, skied the Alps, climbed the Great Wall, raced in bike messenger races in New York and San Francisco.

Lydia is CEO of Venntive.com, the Complete CRM spanning the entire customer lifecycle. She's also launched Tryst @ GirlGroove.com where adults discover new levels of intimacy.

Align

When true to our beliefs and values, we become magnets that align with and for others.

Contact Lydia Sugarman

Venntive.com

917-445-8637

lksugarman@venntive.com

River Easter

River Easter is a catalyst to help you discover the genius inside YOU. More than your average life coach, her vast toolbox includes more than 20 years of neuroscience, smartcuts, paradigm busting. A Masters in Organization Development and is a certified Life Mastery Consultant. Get started on your Aligned Life, with your free Road Map at www.YourAlignedLifeRoadmap.com.

Aligned

The state of being tapped-in, in flow, and congruent with your unique and essential self.

Contact River Easter

River@RiverEaster.com

www.RiverEaster.com

www.instagram.com/RiverTamEaster/

facebook.com/RippleEffectConsulting/

Diane Kale

Diane Kale:
I help people create amazeable health in their life. Through support and education learn easy and effective ways to reach their health goals by creating healthy habits that last a lifetime.

Amazeable

A combination of Amazing and Incredible
Word created by Allie May Scheu

Contact Diane Kale

https://www.diane4health.com

diane4health@yahoo.com

805-405-7969

Lindsay Gledhill

Lindsay has always been a very unique person. He has been a tax professional for the past 30 plus years, but for the past 3 years has stepped out into another world of helping people through encouraging words and engagement in conversations to up lift them to think better of themselves. Search him out and you will find out why!

Amazing

AMAZING is what we each can accomplish if we set our mind to it!

Contact Lindsay Gledhill

https://www.lindsaygledhill.com

lindsay@lindsaygledhill.com

916-792-0387

Elizabeth Trinh

Elizabeth Trinh is a high school student, that has traveled to third-world countries such as Haiti, the Dominican Republic, Vietnam, Peru and Mexico as a Youth Ambassador with several NGO's. There she helped provide clothes, toys, books, basic hygiene, and medical services, under the supervision of physicians and nurses. She is currently the ASB Publicity Director, Key Club President, National Honor Society Member.

Ambitious

Having a passionate desire to achieve large aspirations in life.

Contact Elizabeth Trinh

Elizabethmaitrinh@gmail.com

Janet Nicholson

Janet Nicholson: To be fully alive and/or rich AND very very happy, let's make money doing only what we love. Create teams who love to do what we don't; and the sky's the limit! Finding others with passion, for teams, I like best. (Plus Transpac: Race Long Beach to Honolulu) That can make $$$$$$ too! Ask me!
sailing.copesetic@gmail.com

Amer1can

Individualists' all contributing their gifts, linked by Epluribusunum 'Out of Many One' 1 Nation, 1 people not hyphenated citizens.

Contact Janet Nicholson

555 N Harbor Dr #17
Redondo Beach, CA 90277

310-421-6955

sailing.copesetic@gmail.com

Bridget Brady

Bridget Brady is an entrepreneur, speaker, social media authority and #1 International Bestselling author. Her company, **Amp Up My Biz**, is a leader in the world of online marketing, and provides full-service marketing solutions: **Social Media Marketing & Training, Website Development, and Graphic Design**. Bridget is passionate about helping business owners grow their brands, their businesses and their bottom lines.

Amplify

Be heard! Your message, voice, soul, ringing out to the world. Loud, strong ... un-apologetically YOU.

Contact Bridget Brady

AmpUpMyBiz.com

Facebook.com/AmpUpMyBiz

Twitter.com/AmpUpMyBiz

YouTube.com/AmpUpMyBiz

LinkedIn.com/in/TheBridgetBrady

Instagram.com/AmpUpMyBiz

Pinterest.com/AmpUpMyBiz

Pamela Hoffman

Pam Hoffman, EverydaySpacer.com, is best known for producing National Space Society's International Space Development Conference in Cleveland, Ohio. She's a Space Frontier Foundation Advocate and held positions in several space, astronomy and science organizations. Her favorite preoccupation now is to show regular folks how they too can play in this sandbox!

Analemma

The Sun! Appearing as a figure eight, photographed once a day, from the same location.

Contact Pamela Hoffman

Pam@EverydaySpacer.com

805-590-6356

EverydaySpacer.com

Jeff Miller

Many people have their head so buried in their business that all they see are the problems. I look at your business with a more holistic view to show you how to get your head out of the business and look around for the solutions and opportunities that are all around you. MBA with 28 years of business experience.

Apotheosis

The highest point in the development of something; culmination, or climax. Also, deification.

Contact Jeff Miller

2049Outfitters.com

Jeff@2049Outfitters.com

Carey McClean

Carey McLean is The App Chicks' creator,
technical guru, and designer. Carey is goal
oriented, queen of troubleshooting and
repeatedly gets the job done in the most efficient
manner. As the App Chicks' CEO, her cutting-
edge skills transform her customers' ideas into
reality. It is her acute intuition and swift
implementation that sets Carey apart from the
rest.

Apps

Custom designed mobile and desktop software programs built for a specific business need or purpose.

Contact Carey McClean

www.TheAppChicks.com

Ronald E. Howell

Ronald E. Howell AIA is an architect located in Venice, California. Ron was raised in Venice, Schooled at Cal Poly San Luis Obispo, refined while living in Europe and influenced by traveling the World. Ron is the creator of high end residential and commercial projects throughout Southern California and Hawaii.

Architecture

Architecture is the art of creating environment.

Contact Ronald E. Howell

Ronald E. Howell AIA

REHArchitect.com

310-780-2782

Charese Mongiello

Photo by Shawn Barber

I have always strived to be the best at everything I do and also have fun at the same time. I do that as head of Production at OKTV and in my online blog and school for filmmakers at www.moviemakercentral.com.

Artist

A technician, expert at getting intention across to many; A soul with power to inspire emotions.

Contact Charese Mongiello

www.moviemakercentral.com

951-833-8498

moviemakercentral@gmail.com

Alice March

Alice Aspen March, Author, Speaker, Executive Director of Non-Profit, (lobbyist for quality TV programming for kids, kept Fred Rogers on PBS), appointee by CA State Senate to 2 State Commissions, mother of three sons, grandmother, and a great-grandmother has researched, written, spoken worldwide about the vital role ATTENTION plays in family, business, social, and personal lives.

Attention

WE FEEL, SEE, HEAR, AND SENSE
IT.
IT IS EVERYONE'S CORE ISSUE 24/7.

Contact Alice March

Website: www.TheAttentionFactor.com

Phone: 212-457-1940

Email: alice@theattentionfactor.com

Annette Jacobson

Annette Jacobson is a Business Coach who works with people to find their power and resources to create the business they desire and live the life of their dreams. Her clients are no longer stuck, unhappy, overwhelmed, struggling to grow their businesses. Instead, they've achieved success. Isn't it time you did, too?

Audacious

Courageous, bold, spirited, determined; willing to take risks.

Contact Annette Jacobson

annettebrunojacobson@gmail.com

Patricia Muesse

Through intuitive coaching and hypnosis, I awaken your subconscious to discover the root of what's holding you back. This process addresses the core issue, not the symptom, to create a lasting transformation - from the inside out. I work with people all over the globe, but hang my hat in Santa Barbara, California with my love, a black lab named Rosie.

Authentic

I am Spirit, free of all limits. Perfect joy, love, peace and happiness.

Patricia Muesse, CCHt

Intuitive Coach & Hypnotherapist

Santa Barbara, California

805-883-8595

www.patriciamuesse.com

Norma Hollis

Norma T. Hollis is an international authority on authenticity and self-awareness. She is a coach, consultant, speaker, trainer and author of programs, services and books that help you deepen your knowledge of self, transition difficult times, follow your authentic life path and become a more effective leader.

Authenticity

True to self; putting people and purpose before profit; focusing on the common good.

Contact Norma Hollis

NormaHollis.com

www.AuthenticityU.com

323-734-7144

Jan Fishler

Jan Fishler began her career producing videos, and has written more than 100 corporate scripts. She produced "The Path to Publication" DVD series that contains advice from authors including Amy Tan, Anne Lamott, and Janet Fitch. In 2010, she published *Searching for Jane, Finding Myself (an adoption memoir)*. This year, she co-authored *Don't Stop Now: Making the Most of the Rest of Your Life*.

Author

A writer of books and other print content; ideally a collection of words worth reading.

Contact Jan Fishler

Author - Speaker - Writing Coach

530-277-9173

www.JanFishler.net

www.Don'tStopNow.us

www.facebook.com/DontStopNow.thebook

Joy Willett

Joy Willett has been passionate about personal development for over 30 yrs!

As a Trainer of N.L.P., Hypnosis, and Time Line Therapy®, she enjoys assisting others with her Avatar By Design Programs & training others to help transform this World!

Her book about Joy debuted in Fall 2018!

Avatar

Avatar represents that Highest Version of Oneself. It is Your Light descending to Earth!

Contact Joy Willett

JoysofSuccess.com

949-520-0095

iamjoyworld@gmail.com

Paul Hoyt

Paul Hoyt, President of Hoyt Management Group, CEO of Ascending Harvest, and the founder of the Mind Sequencing System, is passionate about helping others Awaken. He is the author of two business books: The Foundation Factor®, and The Capital Coaching Program, and also the best-selling author of an inspirational book, The First Light of Joy.

Awakening

A sudden, dramatic shift in consciousness that brings greater awareness, wisdom, and love.

Contact Paul Hoyt

www.PaulHoyt.com
paul@paulhoyt.com

Google Voice (finds me): 415-997-8001
Direct Office Line: 408-326-2937

To Set an appointment:
 www.SchedulePaul.com

Facebook: https://www.facebook.com/paul. hoyt
LinkedIn: https://linkedin.com/in/ paulhoyt/en
YouTube: https://youtube.com/user/ paulhoyt

A

Grace Moniz

Grace Moniz, M.S., BCC, executive coach, specializes in personal growth and team dynamics. She supports leaders in accelerating positive change and increasing confidence and compassion. Teams develop a *foundation of common understanding*™ that stimulates alignment, fuels engagement, and unleashes creativity. Clients span aerospace, healthcare, education, consumer products, and air transportation sectors. Grace holds multiple certifications in assessments and coaching methodologies.

Awareness

…awakens a stirring for change…a realization of the possibility for real growth towards your potential.

Contact Grace Moniz

Moniz Executive & Team Coaching

310-800-0333

2121 Rosecrans Ave., Suite 2385
El Segundo, CA 90245

https://calendly.com/gracemoniz/30min

James Poindexter III

James is a former foster kid who went
beastmode on life and became a World Martial
Arts Champion, #1 Best Selling Author,
Entrepreneur and Motivational Speaker.

Beastmode

A focused state of mind when you're giving all you have and letting nothing stop you. You have one goal and that's to be #1.

Contact James Poindexter III

jameshpoindexter.com

415-483-5333

jhbrands@jameshpoindexter.com

Amy M. Goodman

Referred to as a pioneer for women. Amy is the first woman to calibrate professional racecar engines. After more than 20 racing championships she seized the opportunity to move to the human side of business. By day is an automotive manufacturers rep. and consultant. Hobbies: Producing The Landmark Forum, expressing herself though choreographed dance and worldwide adventure travel.

Beautilicious

Beauty so intense that it heightens the taste.

Contact Amy M. Goodman

Amy@AmyGoodmanConsulting.com

https://www.linkedin.com/in/amy-goodman-45b9281/

https://ezcard.com/?8249

Lynn Sanders

Lynn Sanders, Founder/President of Difference Makers Media, is a story expert, providing award-winning writing, marketing consulting, speaking and video interviews to help entrepreneurs build their impact. She hosts "The Difference Makers," a WebTV show, featuring tips from business leaders. Lynn also authored the best-selling children's book, "Dancing With Tex," and "Social Justice: How You Can Make A Difference."

Believe

To see with your heart. Having unconditional faith.

Contact Lynn Sanders

Lynn@DifferenceMakersMedia.com

847-501-2867 (o) or 847-630-1174 (c)

www.DifferenceMakersMedia.com

Stacy Osborne

Stacy is a certified Medicaid planner in Colorado. She has an extensive financial and business background that allows her to understand and correctly assign personal and business assets correctly in order to preserve assets and qualify for Long Term Care Medicaid. Her firms mission statement is summed up in one word.... "BENEFICENT".

Beneficent

DOING GOOD FOR OTHERS.
ACTIONS THAT ARE BENEFICIAL
FOR OTHERS.

Contact Stacy Osborne

Stacy@DoingGoodForOthers.com

www.DoingGoodForOthers.com

719-645-8350

Gladys Monroy Boutwell

An Insurance Broker in Health, Life, Property, and Casualty for Oregon and Washington. MBA in International Business and Leadership & Management from University of La Verne, Six Sigma Green Belt Certified through Microsoft, and a Certified Insurance Counselor (CIC).

"Madrina de Salud" award recipient for contributions to Latino equity and Amazon's #1 Best Selling author for her book "Health Insurance Secrets Revealed".

Benefits

Employer-paid (monetary, non-cash, or indirect) compensation in addition to wages to recruit, retain, and reward.

Contact Gladys M. Boutwell, MBA, CIC

503-223-3638

gboutwell@whainsurance.com

www.whainsurance.com

2930 Chad Dr, Eugene, OR 97408

Lauren Hammond

Lauren Hammond worked in the entertainment field before venturing into the corporate world. With 20+ years of experience helping nonprofits raise money through her former company, Sporthings & More, Lauren branched out on her own and started Creative Charity Auctions LLC. She understands what makes an auction successful and enjoys working with clients to ensure their needs are met.

Bighearted

I raise money for nonprofits by providing unique items for their silent and live auctions.

Contact Lauren Hammond

creativecharityauctions.com

818-840-1200

laurenh@creativecharityauctions.com

Paul Michael Dekker

Paul-Michael is a Systems Design Engineer, futurist and writes on specific technical projects. He is a Founder of <u>Green Star Standard</u>, an environmental impact consultancy.

Past Member of: SASC, sustainable community policy advocates and SDRSP, IEEE, & IMC (San Diego Chapter).

He joined <u>GENI</u> in 1993 & speaks about GENI, *SIM*<u>Center,</u> & blockchain technology.

Bitcoin

First digital peer-to-peer cryptocurrency where blockchain technology generated tokens, coins, and verified value transfers.

Contact Paul Michael Dekker

Web: www.greenblockchains.com

Phone: +1-619-595-0158

Email: info@greenblockchains.com

LinkedIn:
www.linkedin.com/in/paulmichaeldekker

Brands:
Byte Butler, Global Subscribe, and
Team Dynamo

Rosemary "Ro" Glassman

I have been married for 27 years and have 3 beautiful children. I lost myself 5 years ago and got a second chance with Touchstone Crystal. I'm an introvert, but you wouldn't know it. I raise a lot of money doing fundraisers. I'm all about CHANGING LIVES and empowering women. Love yourself!

Bling

Swarovski Crystal! Sparkle inside & out.
Feel alive. Make a STATEMENT! Be
UNIQUE! Be YOU!!

Contact Ro Glassman

Touchstone Crystal
by Swarovski Jewelry

732-614-6361

www.touchstonecrystal.com/Ro

GrabMyJewelsByRo@gmail.com

Facebook~Touchstone Crystal By
Swarovski with RO

Norissa Rochelle Cuyno Ennis

Rissa is a SoCal native and youngest of six with a Hawaiian heritage. She enjoys creativity; singing, writing and fine arts. She was an avid and competitive athlete; cross country, track, basketball, tennis, softball and volleyball. Rissa was married and diagnosed with breast cancer both in 2004, and since then has blissfully walked through her wonderful life with her husband Eric.

Blissfully

Light on your feet; simple happiness;
living without a care in the world.

Contact Norissa Rochelle Cuyno Ennis

Rissa Cuyno Ennis

RED Concept LLC
174 W. Lincoln Ave. Suite 516
Anaheim, CA 92805

949-322-1771

rissa@redconcept-usa.com

redconcept-usa.com

Terri Rose

Terri Rose is a Love & Lifestyle Coach and National Speaker committed to serving those in life transitions of separation and divorce. After leaving her 13 year marriage, she has walked the emotionally challenging path of divorce. With a strong and passionate desire to serve and empower others, she brings unique insight and inspiration from her own life experiences.

Blissify™

Creating a state of pure happiness, Bliss
from a heart centered place of Self-Love.

Contact Terri Rose

Love & Lifestyle Coach with
Blissify Your Life™

Blissifyyourlife.com

916-425-8383

Love@Blissifyyourlife.com

Tim Gillette

Tim Gillette is the creator of Simple Easy Marketing, a blog, video, and online content creation system designed to get results with your online marketing, even if you're new to it.

Tim's an award winning blogger and #1 Amazon Best Selling Author. He lives in Dallas with his wife, Gwynne, cat, Sefu and 3 adult children.

Blog

A simple easy way to market your business and turn quality traffic into sales.

Contact Tim Gillette

www.timgillette.com

info@timgillette.com

Roberta Perry

Roberta Perry is a Business Development specialist currently working with Edwards Technologies, Inc. (ETI)   She has served as Chairman of the Nightclub and Bar Association; as President of the Themed Entertainment Association; sat on Seattle Fair Campaign and Practices Commission; International Board Director for Toastmasters International and currently serves on the Board for Lawrence Anthony's Earth Organization.

Bodacious

A fun word that rolls off the tongue meaning bold and audacious.

Contact Roberta Perry

www.robertaperry.com

roberta.perry1@gmail.com

310-709-2613

Lillian Freeman

Lillian Freeman, LCSW is a psychotherapist in private practice in West Los Angeles. She specializes in Family therapy, Addiction treatment, Couples therapy, Healthy Aging, and Career transitions. Her wholistic approach comes from 35 years of experience as a psychotherapist and Adjunct College Professor. She has taught and lectured throughout the state of California.

Bounce-back

What if the technology is now available to reset your Brain to balance your body?

Contact Lillian Freeman

Integrative Family Center
Lillian Freeman, LCSW

12304 Santa Monica Blvd. suite 215
Los Angeles, Calif.90025

310-440-1963

lillianfreemanlcsw@earthlink.net

Susan Hutchins

Find out more about Susan Hutchins by
contacting her at: miracles111@gmail.com

Brain-on

What if the technology is now available to reset your Brain to balance your body.

Contact Susan Hutchins

miracles1111@gmail.com

480-696-3800

Ashley Roda

Clients call me "The Persona Stylist." I provide creative direction and project management for business owners looking to bring consistency, cohesion and charisma to their branding and marketing. My specialty is identifying the details that make my clientele iconic and memorable.

Branding

Your ability to differentiate and exemplify the unique value you bring to your industry.

Contact Ashley Roda

Founder & Creative Director, Iconic Details

541-301-6554

Ashley@IconicDetails.com

www.IconicDetails.com

Janet K. Fish

A reformed corporate executive turned serial entrepreneur, I have found my passion in coaching others. I've been coaching entrepreneurs since 2005, helping people start or grow their business, make lots of money and invest it for long-term growth and security.

Breakaway

The art of breaking away from the pack. Setting yourself apart from your competition.

Contact Janet K. Fish

Breakaway Business Coaching

https://BreakawayBusinessCoaching.com

janet@breakawayllc.com

775-285-7325

Tobi Brown

Tobi Brown started her career as a software engineer and went on to excel in several roles with increasing responsibility at a Washington, DC trade association. Tobi now serves as Founder of Curated Brilliance® Consulting where she is helping partners to identify their ideal clients, deliver on their brand promises, and launch projects and programs to serve their audiences.

Brilliance

Divine expression of whatever a person or thing is created to be or to do.

Contact Tobi Brown

Tobi Brown,
Founder, Curated Brilliance® Consulting Services

Email: tobi@curatedbrilliance.com

Web: https://curatedbrilliance.com

Facebook: @curatedbrilliance

Joanne Neweduk

Nurturing others to holistic health, effectively rekindling their light of joy, has inspired mastermind leader and wellness innovator, Joanne Neweduk, to enhance her nursing education with the modalities, light and sound therapy, belief re-patterning and personal leadership coaching, essential for her clients' success in breaking through the blockages impeding their body's self-healing process. **When you are pain-free, everything is possible!**

Brilliant

Outstanding, incandescent, extraordinary!
Free of fear, undaunted by doubt,
empowered, unique and authentic, we
SHINE!!!

Contact Joanne Neweduk

Joanne Neweduk,
Founder Brilliant Light Wellness

www.BrilliantLightWellness.com

Joanne@BrilliantLightWellness.com

Amy James

I am Amy James and I am the owner of Amy's Social Butterfly, I make handmade 3D greeting cards. I am from Dallas, TX and I enjoy making people smile and this is why. I began making these special greeting cards for everyone to enjoy and hopefully bring a smile to their face.

Butterfly

Butterfly to me means strength, courage and determination to go on in spite of all odds.

Contact Amy James

Website: www.AmysSocialButterfly.com

Email: Info@AmysSocialButterfly.com

Phone: 469-835-1655

Facebook Business page:
Facebook.com/AmysSocialButterlyLLC

Instagram: AmysSocialButterfly.com

Twitter: @AmysSocialB

Darlene Basch

Darlene Basch, LCSW utilizes body psychotherapy successfully helping hundreds of people overcome daily anxiety, post-traumatic stress and other life challenges. She specializes in working with families, children, teens, and millennials, addressing parenting, sexual abuse, dysfunctional relationships, Holocaust issues and spiritual dilemmas. Darlene is a Board-Certified Diplomate in Clinical Social Work, and a Certified Practitioner/Teacher of Integrative Body Psychotherapy.

Calm

Welcome to the World of Calm - Feel grounded, present, in your body, relaxed, serene, at peace.

Contact Darlene Basch

transformationtherapy.com

323-937-4974

darlene@transformationtherapy.com

Cynthia Stone

Cynthia helps people design their destiny...
having created her career out of nothing but
persistence, passion and purpose. She's a host
on The Disability Channel and has dedicated her
life to serving others. From the ghettos to
Guyana, from the shelters to the shut-ins, and
from Fort Mac and back, she is driven to help
people live a life in line with their Divine.

Canerican

A cross between Canadian and American. Spending ample time in both Canada and US can result in Canerican status.

Contact Cynthia Stone

https://m.imdb.com/name/nm6289776/

https://www.facebook.com/iamtheoriginal cyn/

Instagram: @_cyndiana_stone

Iamtheoriginalcyn.com (coming soon)

Phone: 416-856-8084

Iamtheoriginalcyn@gmail.com

Dave Nassaney

DAVE NASSANEY is a speaker, radio host, life-coach and best-selling author of, **"It's My Life, Too! Reclaim Your Caregiver Sanity."** However, his most important role is caregiver to his lovely wife, Charlene, who suffered a massive stroke in 1996 that left her severely speech-impaired and paralyzed on the right side.

Caregiver

Provision of what is necessary for the health, welfare, maintenance, & protection of someone you love.

Contact Dave Nassaney

CaregiverDave.com

661-904-5060

Dave@Nassaney.TV

C

Samantha Grier a.k.a. Shulamit Sofia

SAMANTHA GRIER MSW, the Founder and President of CARING FOR CHILDREN has received the CBS Jefferson Award and been nominated to be a CNN Hero because of her extensive work on behalf of traumatized children. She is the author of "Psalms for a Sunny Day" and "Climbing The Sacred Ladder: Your Path to Love Joy Peace and Purpose" under her pen name Shulamit Sofia.

Caring

Compassion in Action.

Contact Samantha Grier
a.k.a.
Shulamit Sofia

Samantha Grier, MSW

Samantha@caringforchildren.org

Shulamit Sofia

shulamitsofia@soulstrengthseminars.com

C

Kevin E. West

<u>Kevin E. West</u> is a veteran television actor, public speaker and author (*Kevin's Dictionary: 'Life In A Word' & 7 Deadly Sins: The Actor Overcomes*) originally from rural Nashville, who affectionately calls himself, *The Hollywood Redneck*. His credits include Guest Stars on *Aquarius, Criminal Minds, Bones, Castle, CSI: Miami, Justified, Leverage, Lost, 24, NCIS, Alias, CSI, n'* dozens more. Cheers, @theKevinE

Chameleon

To effortlessly pass between the raindrops of life while maximizing one's strength & achieving peak engagement.

Contact Kevin E. West

Email: kevin@kevinewest.com

Cell: 818-389-9585

Web: www.kevinewest.com

Mailing: 11684 Ventura Blvd. - #757, Studio City, CA 91604

C

Mellissa Tong

A TV Newscaster turned award-winning director/producer in films, documentaries, and TV commercials, Mellissa's worked with Fortune 500 companies and won many awards including The Clio, Addy, Telly, and others. Her storytelling skills has helped her clients grow their business by more than 70%. Now, she devotes 25% of her time to help entrepreneurs "tell their stories and be a rock star on camera."

Change

Change is never easy, but I believe it is absolutely necessary, for your own evolution.

Contact Mellissa Tong

310-627-8666

mellissa@duckpunk.net

mellissatong.com

duckpunk.net

rockstaroncamera.com

Sharon Weil

Sharon Weil is the author of ChangeAbility, How Artists, Activists and Awakeners Navigate Change and ChangeAbility Playbook, How to Navigate Your Own Change, books designed to help readers effectively navigate all the changes in their lives. Sharon also authored the humorous novel, Donny and Ursula Save the World, and is the host of Passing 4 Normal Podcast, conversations about change.

ChangeAbility

The ability to effectively navigate change with greater flexibility and ease.

Contact Sharon Weil

sharonweilauthor.com

310-459-3326

sharonweilauthor@gmail.com

www.facebook.com/authorsharonweil/

C

Frances Pullin

Frances began to channel Amadeus Mozart in 2007. She channels other energies, but he is her main guide. He has told her he has come to repay Karma from their lifetime together as siblings in the 1700's. Frances is a medium, intuitive and hypnotherapist and practices in Orange County, CA and Tucson, AZ.

Channeling

Moving Ego out, consciousness is raised to allow spirit to bring forth messages of wisdom.

Contact Frances Pullin

Francespullin.com

frances@francespullin.com

francespullin@gmail.com

714-904-8395

C

P.K. Odle

P.K. Odle is a Master Feng Shui Consultant and Executive Director of the renowned *American Feng Shui Institute®*, where she's taught since 1998. Her consultations and revolutionary 'Personal Directions Self-Mastery Toolbox' teaches clients how manage their unique 15° Magnetic Directions that affect their entire life. She privately evaluates/consults on existing structures and project development for residential and commercial clients worldwide.

Chi/QI

Chinese name for the Universal Life-Force Energy which can be changed, but not created or destroyed.

Contact P.K. Odle

The Feng Shui Advantage®

626-288-1669

www.PKFengShui.com

PK@PKFengShui.com

C

Phyllis Keitlen

In the 70's/80's, she was an innovative Knitwear designer. Her cool t-shirts, knits, "Vogue" she created " The Italian TRUCK DRIVER'S T-SHIRT into fashion chic must halves."

Managed Jose Feliciano, accompanying him world-wide.

Created Savvy Chic, Inc-Made in the USA; Organic Shea Butter, Exotic Oils, Body Butter Creams, and more, with rejuvenating healing powers. And CousCous Doggy Shampoo and Pet Paws Cream.

Chic

Elegant, Savvy, Creative, Stylish,
Tasteful, Breath Taking, Wow,
Spectacular, Gorgeous, Charismatic,
Effortless, Sparkle, Caring, Glamping.

Contact Phyllis Keitlen

www.sochicnyc.com

212-744-0455

phyllis@sochicnyc.com

C

Deeann Elder

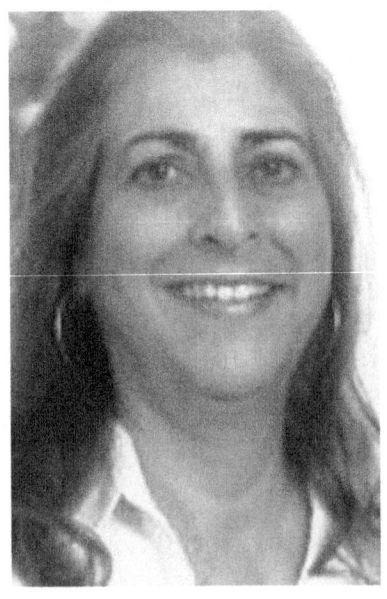

Deeann Elder has been in the nutrition world for over twenty five years. She shares her knowledge about the benefits of Healthy Chocolate with others so they can be happier, healthier and live longer. She has taught classes to hundreds of college students and is a bestselling author.

Chocolate

Eating delicious healthy chocolate every day can help you be happier, healthier and live longer.

Contact Deeann Elder

Health and Happiness,
Beyond Healthy Chocolate

deeannelder.com

949-302-1130

C

Nykki Hardin

Nykki Hardin a professional psychic medium and the formulator of 21 Cleanse, her proprietary blend, therapeutic grade, organic detox program to help get the toxins out of the body without fasting, starving, or sacrificing your lifestyle. She holds a masters in Spiritual Psychology and is passionate about helping people transform inside and out thru full body cleansing and tools of self-mastery.

Cleanse

To let go physically, mentally, emotionally and spiritually of that which does not serve.

Contact Nykki Hardin

www.nykkihardin.com

C

Linda L. Johnson

Linda Johnson works with individuals and small groups, helping them build their dreams, accelerate their results, and create richer, more fulfilling lives. Bringing over 39 years of successful experience in the business world and the school of life, Linda's work is focused on serving others in their journey of living their life by design versus default.

Coach

A person who guides and supports clients in discovering and creating their dreams.

Contact Linda L. Johnson

Life Coach

805-233-0748

www.LindaJohnsonLifeCoach.com

linda@LindaJohnsonLifeCoach.com

C

Melanie Fatuesi

Melanie Fatuesi, DTM hales from Swartz Creek, Michigan. She joined the Army at 18 and has traveled the world, serving from Somalia to Guantanamo to Korea. Melanie has one son, Luka who recently graduated from and works for Stanford University and she resides on the west side of El Paso.

Coffee

Coffee is the meaning of Life - Coffee keeps you moving at the speed of Business.

Contact Melanie Fatuesi

www.succeedachievelead.com

Melanie.Fatuesi@gmail.com

915-503-7274

C

Terri Hardin

International speaker, artist, Jim Henson Puppeteer and Walt Disney's Legendary Imagineer Terri's "Cash In Your Passion," teaches you to use innovation to elevate your business or to make a living doing what you love.

She's designed attractions all over the world. Her films include. Men In Black, Ghostbusters, and more. She's funny, upbeat and tells great stories. Google me and see.

Collaboration

When like-minded people put their egos
aside and come together as a team
creating magic.

Contact Terri Hardin

www.terrihardin.com

C

Denise Schickel, Ph.D.

Denise has been developing self-care practices and pursuing greater understanding for many years. She has studied and practiced various bodywork modalities, along with yoga. Her current studies in psychology have been valuable as well.

Her relationship to commitment during her journey has been tested and strengthened by obstacles placed in her path.

Commitment

Commitment is your Foundation,
It Drives you, Feeds you,
Surrounds you, and
Creates your Context.

Contact Denise Schickel, Ph.D.

www.SelfCareExpert.com

C

Scott Schilling

Scott Schilling is the Co-Founder of YouPlus1.com, a committed community where people care about, for, and support each other in realizing their dreams! Scott personally is committed to providing Inspired Answers to Today's Challenges through his TV Show, Podcasts, speaking, training, consulting and coaching. Scott helps individuals and organizations systematically grow personally, professionally, financially and spiritually.

Community

...Committed group where people care about, for, and support each other in realizing their dreams!

Contact Scott Schilling

YouPlus1.com

844-955-SAVE (7283)

Scott@YouPlus1.com

c

Kathy Pendleton

Kathy Pendleton is a best-selling author, an international award-winning speaker, and a compassionate patient advocate.

Her fifteen plus years of providing patient care during family illnesses have taught her that no one cares more about your health or your family's health than you do.

Speak up to get the care your loved one deserves.

Compassion

A sympathetic awareness of another person's distress along with a desire to alleviate it. This emotion fuels my connection to my clients!

Contact Kathy Pendleton

www.GetTheCareYouDeserve.com

C

Miles Berdache Lynk

I am just an average man who had to persevere
through great adversity in order to realize how
truly exceptional I am. No degrees or flammable
proof of laborious study, just a simple, lifelong,
journey to overcome addictions, childhood
trauma, low self worth and sexual stigma. I *am*
Divine Energy of Light, *just like you.*

Concierge

One who holds the key and lights the way toward a desired destination.

Contact Miles Berdache Lynk

5905 Pine View Dr.
Paradise, California 95969

(c) 530-826-6862

(o) 800-351-9904

www.readysuccessgo.com

C

Andrea Spyros

Owner of one of LA's Top 25 Gift Shops, Andrea Spyros is inspired to create a new way of being in business where community is a priority and employees love what they do and where they are doing it. When she's not immersing herself in new research, you can find her painting mandalas or playing bass guitar.

Confidence

Knowing, deep down, without a doubt: YOU GOT THIS!

Contact Andrea Spyros

AndreaSpyros.com

Andrea@AndreaSpyros.com

Facebook.com/Andrea.Spyros

C

Abe Serrano

Abe Serrano is a premier Real Estate & Business Advisor who specializes in combining his knowledge of Real Estate and experience with financing to assist Cannabis and Health care professionals in the Selling and Buying of Cannabis and Healthcare related Businesses and Real Estate. He assists established healthcare professionals expand their businesses while helping others downsize to different endeavors.

Connector

Master Connector in cannabis & Healthcare. Facilitating deals to come together for the Benefit of All!

Contact Abe Serrano

Email: abeser@gmail.com

Cell phone: 818-200-8067

C

Rhona Jordan

Guided Imagery Therapist, Medical & Dental
Hypnosis, Reiki Master, Global Primordial
Sound Meditation Instructor for Dr. Deepak
Chopra, Humanitarian of the Year Award,
Published Author: Your Amazing Itty Bitty
Imagery Book, Your Amazing Itty Bitty
Meditation Book, Your Amazing Itty Bitty
Interstitial Cystitis Book. Serving IHF
International Hypnosis Federation Board of
Advisers & TOSS Thoracic Outlet Syndrome
Society Board of Advisers.

Consciousness

Is everywhere, like the atom it is explosive with expanding creative forces and potentially.

Contact Rhona Jordan

714-974-4094

www.Rhonaimagery.com

Rhonaimagery@aol.com

Guided Imagery Therapist

C

Sonja M. Talley

Sonja M. Talley, provides coaching and Human Resouces consulting services. She serves on the Arizona HR Board (AZSHRM) and her education includes a HeartMath coaching certification, a BA in business administration and a master's in human resources as well as doctoral studies in Industrial/ Organizational Psychology. Her personal time is spend with family, yoga, and nature.

Core

Heart Foundation at the center of being;
Competence - Compliance - Compassion

Contact Sonja M. Talley

CORE HR Solutions, LLC

602-459-0063

sonjamtalley@gmail.com

C

Sonia Shafazand

Sonia immigrated to the USA, working full time and going to school while a single mom of two toddlers; she has learned how to be authentically happy. She holds a Masters and works with executives, professionals, entrepreneurs, stay at home moms and students. She gets a profound sense of joy when clients report and thank her for their breakthroughs and happiness.

Courage

This makes everything possible; especially living a happy and authentic life, by moving through fear.

Contact Sonia Shafazand

Trusted Advisor, Life Coach & Mentor to those who choose to have a Better, Happier Life NOW.

Email: sonia@Shafazand.com

Website: BandOfCourage.com

Phone: 408-605-9694

C

Vivian Geffen

Vivian Geffen helps people overcome their
discomfort of being the center of attention by
teaching skills that increase confidence in their
ability to be heard, connect with others and think
on their feet. She leads Creative Thinking and
Improvisation workshops and recently partnered
with Equinox to introduce a fitness +
improvisation class. She has a master's degree
in Creativity from SUNY Buffalo.

Creativity

Team up-
Generate questions.
See new connections.
Engage different perspectives.
Reflect, rearrange, create and iterate.

Contact Vivian Geffen

http://www.creativitymuse.com

323-206-6131

vivian@creativitymuse.com

facebook.com/creativeproblemsolving

Debe Bloom

Debe Bloom resides in Ventura County and enjoys being a mobile entrepreneur with her husband (www.DebeAndRick.com) She is a member of Women in Technology, National Association of Female Executives, among other organizations and was awarded the Women Entrepreneur Business Award of Excellence in 2011. She is an active volunteer in community activities.

Credibility

To stand tall knowing you represent the best 'you' possible where trust & respect prevail.

Contact Debe Bloom

415-713-9030

debe@debeandrick.com

www.DebeAndRick.com

C

Laurel Rolls

Laurel INSPIRES her clients to discover their own POSSIBILITIES and pursue them NOW! Her strong intuition, insightfulness and CURIOSITY supports her clients in creating their own unique fabric of possibilities and creative actions. Laurel guides her clients through awareness of limiting beliefs and behaviors – the landmines keeping them from success and happiness –and eliminate them!

Curiosity

CURIOSITY opens our minds and lives to infinite possibilities, understanding, connection, learning and JOY!

Contact Laurel Rolls

Laurel@LaurelRolls.com

www.TheConnectionLanguage.com

214-770-3854

Kathleen Peake

Kathy Peake is a graduate of Mary Washington College with a BS in Chemistry. An Independent Financial Advisor for 17 years, providing investment and insurance services in Arizona and Colorado, she is creator of the popular, MY MONEY ADVENTURE workshop. Kathy serves as Managing Director of the Northern Colorado Chapter of eWomenNetwork when she is not being an amazing grandmother.

Currency

Dynamic circulation or exchange of money, trade, or connection; continual flow of energy and power.

Contact Kathleen Peake,
Financial Advisor

www.mymoneyadventure.com

520-661-8467

kathy@mymoneyadventure.com

Greeley, Colorado

C

Maria Fontaine

I turned my pain into my Purpose, Damsel in Defense - My Passion is to help women stay safe with confidence

We have the tools to help you feel secure. My Goal is to Equip, Empower & Educate women on self defense

Damsel is about 'Staging' your home, work or play area as well as your travels.

Defense

Ware & Layer your protection, Pepper Spray, Stun Gun, and use them with confidence.

Contact Maria Fontaine

Damsel4Safety.com

562-858-3432

marias247store@me.com

Denise Irwin

After my corporate accounting career, I decided to truly help people feel better in their bodies and their lives. I am now a Holistic Health Coach and Essential Oils teacher, teaching people to use Essential Oils and habit change to bring health and freedom to their lives. I am delighted in my work every day!

Delight

Delight fills me with love and light and freedom! Life delights me!

Contact Denise Irwin

Certified Holistic Health Coach

Certified Transformation Coach

doTerra Wellness Advocate

818-524-0181

d.lightmehhc@gmail.com

my.doterra.com/deniseirwin1211

Jimmy Tran

Jimmy Tran is a digital marketing strategist & entrepreneur. His background in computer science, business and marketing helps his clients fused together technology with marketing to reach more customers. At an early age, his work at NASA/JPL and later in the private sector gave him a unique perspective about technology and marketing. Contact him to help you amplify your message.

Digital

The ability to reach more people with your message at a fraction of the cost.

Contact Jimmy Tran

http://WayBeyondSocial.com

505-322-6188

info@WayBeyondSocial.com

Facebook.com/WayBeyondSocial

Christine Lapidus

My clients build financial balance, protecting their families, and businesses from the many threats to their financial wellbeing. I help teach them to protect, save, invest and grow their resources so that they can have – "A Good Life, For the Rest of Your Life."

Disorganancial

The financial products you've accumulated that don't work together to efficiently increase wealth.

Contact Christine Lapidus

christine_lapidus@pacificadvisors.com

818-920-8395

www.pacificadvisors.com/clapidus

Shauna Grace

Shauna Grace is an Internationally top ranked Psychic Medium, and Empowering Empath Specialist and Speaker. She has worked with top leaders and CEO's of Corporations, NFL, and A-list Celebrities. She unleashes access to one's own intuition to create profound breakthroughs in owning one's autonomy and their power to create impact. She too, can do this for you.

Divinity

The Infinite Light and Sacred Essence of your soul that is inherently- WHO YOU BE.

Contact Shauna Grace

www.ShaunaGrace.com

Phone: 360-213-5732

E-mail theshaunagrace@gmail.com

Social Media @theshaunagrace

Justin Recla

Justin Recla has over 14 years of experience as a Counterintelligence Special Agent and Army soldier. He's a subject matter expert in tactical questioning, counter espionage, threat assessments, and investigative techniques. Justin brings his skills from the military sector and delivers them to the boardroom to help business owners and investors protect their two most valuable assets: Time & Money.

Dominion

A level of awareness you achieve when you take responsibility for everything in your life.

Contact Justin Recla

ClearBusinessDirectory.com

Justin@ReclaGroup.com

Amelia Canaya Carpenter

Amelia is an aspiring author and illustrator. All illustrations in her publications she makes herself. Amelia has started a website fourrunesoneworld.com, a blog about a fantasy world she has created herself. She is in process of publishing several books, including "Ruler of Lindelin". Publishing her books is another step in her journey toward a happy, healthy, successful life, alongside her amazing boyfriend and supportive family.

Dream

Something thought to be mere fiction that can come true in the most amazing ways.

Contact Amelia Canaya Carpenter

www.FourRunesOneWorld.com

415-465-9749

Runesandabit@gmail.com

Sherry Turner

Sherry is a wife, mother and grandmother with a background in corporate retail and community volunteerism. While her daughters were growing up Arbonne stepped into her life. She knew immediately that she'd found purity and performance and a decision to partner with Arbonne and build a multi-million dollar home-based business.

Dreamer

To lose oneself in thoughts, images, and feelings and imagine all that is possible.

Contact Sherry Turner

www.sherryturner.arbonne.com

310-266-0412

Sherrylivewell@gmail.com

www.facebook.com/sherry.turner.790

Instagram:Sherrylivewell

Deborah Morgan

Debbie Morgan, CPA is the founder of Deborah Morgan and Company Inc., a full-service tax and accounting firm. Her company caters to entrepreneurs, individuals, as well as non-profits. Debbie is passionate about educating new business owners and helping them overcome their tax and accounting fears so they may focus on their passion – growing their business.

Drive

Motivation and fire to realize your dreams

Contact Deborah Morgan, CPA

805-496-2828

www.DeborahMorganAndCompany.com

Megan DeGonzalez

Hello, my name is Megan DeGonzalez, and my word is Ease. When I'm in a state of ease, life's much better for me. I am the creator of the Three Wisest Monkeys, and that's one of their teachings: to just be. Monkeys & website are getting a makeover, & making a comeback in 2019!

Ease

A Resistant free state; place of simple allowing, absent of any struggle or effort.

Contact Megan DeGonzalez

monkeybiznez.com

828-280-5521

megnd3@gmail.com

E

Didi Wong

Born in Hong Kong, raised in England, and now residing in Los Angeles, Didi Wong is an award winning international speaker, serial entrepreneur and angel investor with expertise in the industries of entrepreneur education, event planning, public speaking, mentoring, interior design and real estate. Didi loves life with her husband and four children, including a set of identical twins.

Edutainment

A blend of education and entertainment.

Contact Didi Wong

www.didiwong.com

917-907-1044

didi@didiwong.com.

Natasha Duswalt

Natasha Duswalt is the owner and founder of Peak Models & Talent In Los Angeles. Natasha Duswalt is also a speaker and author of several books including her latest releases and Amazon Bestsellers ...Women Who Rock and Women Who Rock 2... Inspirational stories of success by extraordinary women!

Elevate

To raise, lift or inspire, enhance, exalt to raise to a higher level position or state.

Contact Natasha Duswalt

www.peakmodels.com

818-889-8800

E

Linda Hansen, Ph.D.

Linda Hansen, PhD, is the CEO and Co-founder of Fund Duel, a revolutionary gamified/competitive online fundraising site that supports a multitude of worthy causes. Linda has co-founded two non-profit organizations. Linda is currently authoring two books and is a co-editor of a scholarly volume on human sacrifice in ancient Mesoamerica.

Elsie

Social Media posts that are altruistic and concern someone else. Antonym: "Selfie" (self-absorbed/narcissistic).

Contact Linda Hansen, Ph.D.

linda@fundduel.com

310-819-5687

E

Lorrie Kazan

Lorrie was chosen as one of the top psychics by Edgar Cayce's Association for Research & Enlightenment.
Praise for her work:
"Lorrie told me I was pregnant the same day (I later learned) I conceived my daughter."
Christine Kloser,
"One 15-min reading saved me $4,500." Janet S.
"Amazed: Lorrie you've been right about everything!" Joan M.

Empath

One who feels your thoughts and feelings often before you do.

Contact Lorrie Kazan

www.ilovemypsychic.com

310-376-5742

E

Barbara Starley

Barbara Starley is a CPA, Christian business owner, author, speaker, wife, and mom. She is passionate about simplifying complex concepts, making QuickBooks® quicker, and empowering small business owners to run their business "by the numbers", so they can become more profitable.

Empower

Empowering others doesn't diminish your value; it increases the value of others to the world.

Contact Barbara Starley, CPA

Website: https://barbarastarley.com/

Phone: 480-251-5291

Email: BarbStarOncall@msn.com

E

Mooniek Seebregts & Martina Caviezel

Being a parent challenges us to the core, our children push every possible button! Let us help you be the mom or dad you imagined you would be! The 7-week course, Great Parents Empower, helps parents develop emotional intelligence, calmness, and ease, it helps them to truly feel empowered. Parent Empowerment coaches Martina & Mooniek have effectively supported parents since 2002!

Empowered

Confident, loving, capable.
In order to raise empowered kids, parents
need to also feel empowered!

Contact Mooniek Seebregts &
Marina Caviezel

info@GreatParentsEmpower.com

GreatParentsEmpower.com

415-848-9013

ℰ

Daphne Marina

Daphne Marina, aka "Goddess Nxt Door" brings her absolutely contagious 1000 watt smile and personality everywhere! Motivator, Speaker and Author, she leads others to FUN--living out their dreams, becoming happier, more confident BE-INGS whom access their imagination, feeling their visions manifest, and experiencing their true power. That's Energy!

Energy

Infinite Yes Energy empowers others to vibrate their value to the universe.

Contact Daphne Marina

CEO Yesmedia

310-853-2678

Social Media:

LinkedIn: Daphne Marina

Facebook: Daphne Marina

Instagram: Daphne.Marina

$\mathcal{E}$

Meryl Ivy Schaffer

Meryl has been a QuickBooks Desktop
Consultant for 19 years. A BS & MS in
Accounting has provided a solid educational
foundation. My understanding of how numbers
work gives me a key sense to the proper
handling/reporting. Nurturing/protecting is
needed for seniors and/or adult disabled people
& individuals who are too busy with other
aspects of their lives.

Enervate

Cause (someone) to feel drained of energy or vitality, weaken. Exhaust, tire, fatigue, weary, devitalize, sap.

Contact Meryl Ivy Schaffer

www.TLCDailyMoneyMentor.com

(O) 301-260-7428

(C) 240-338-3332

(F) 301-260-7429

&

Janie Becker, CMT

Janie Becker focuses on listening to caregivers' needs and helping them heal their physical and emotional traumas using aromatherapy and massage techniques. She is active in the community volunteering to support cancer research and children's' charities. Contact her to subscribe to the monthly Caregivers Corner newsletter to get your free e-book for caregiver strategies at www.lessbrainstressnow.com.

enLIGHTenment

EnLIGHTenment is the state of wisdom and understanding from focused awareness.

Contact Janie Becker, the Encourager

Website: www.lessbrainstressnow.com

Email: aromatherapyplus@verizon.net

Phone: 562-728-8178   M-F 8-6 pst

Giovanna Dottore

Giovanna lights the fire for opportunities in processes and people. She plays at Mattel toys with 19+ years of experience across merchandising, retail sales/marketing/operations, process improvement, change management, training and public speaking. Giovanna is a Toastmasters Past District 1 Governor and a 2013 TEDx Youth Bommer Canyon Conference speaker coach. She dabbles in voice over and founded "Joy Through Toys."

Enrapture

When you surrender to the captivating embrace of being swept off your feet.

Contact Giovanna Dottore

www.giovannadottore.com

giovanna@giovannadottore.com

E

Emily Katz

Emily Katz, is an award winning Make-Up Artist, Image Strategist, and Elle Beauty Genius. She is known in the film and television industry for her informative and inspiring approach to natural beauty. Emily inspires others to embrace their greatness and stand in their beauty. She has been featured in Elle, Marie Claire, InStyle, Glamour, French Glamour, People and InTouch magazines.

Enthusiasum

Embracing the zest and full joy of life-
then sharing that compassionate loving for
whatever you're doing- with world .

Contact Emily Katz

EK Truth

www.ektruth.com

www.eekatz.com

$\mathcal{E}$

Charles Byrd

"The Chaos Killer" - A Silicon Valley veteran.
Deep background in productivity, joint ventures,
and lead flow systems to close more deals.
Reveals secrets that will organize your team,
reduce your anxiety, and x2 your business.

Evernote

Kill the Chaos of Information overload.
Put your finger on anything in 5 seconds.

Contact Charles Byrd

http://i.killthechoas.pro

http://www.Pureflow.pro

415-413-7208

success@killthechoas.pro

P.K. Odle

P.K. Odle is a Master Feng Shui Consultant and Executive Director of the renowned *American Feng Shui Institute®*, where she's taught since 1998. Her consultations and revolutionary 'Personal Directions Self-Mastery Toolbox' teaches clients how manage their unique 15° Magnetic Directions that affect their entire life. She privately evaluates/consults on existing structures and project development for residential and commercial clients worldwide.

Expertise

Mastering a subject through knowledge, skill, competency and experience thus becoming a recognized industry authority.

Contact P.K. Odle

The Feng Shui Advantage®

626-288-1669

www.PKFengShui.com

PK@PKFengShui.com

E

Sara Sas

Specializing in Beauty Medicine: Cosmetic
Facial Acupuncture, Internal Medicine, Yoga
and Face Reading. Over 20 years experience in
Holistic Health Healing Arts, 30 years in Group
Fitness Leadership, Masters in Science and
Traditional Chinese Medicine. Licensed
Acupuncturist -Herbalist-Certified Face Reader-
Certified Aroma-therapist. Sacred Movement-
Yoga Fitness Leader Business owner of Holistic
Traditions Acupuncture Healing Arts Clinic in
La Jolla, CA established 2002.

Face

Appearance Action Expression - BEST FACE FORWARD. The mask of integrity revealed in the countenance constitution.

Contact Sara Sas

www.holistictraditions.com

www.beautyalchemylife.com

619-251-6549 cell

858-551-1005 office

sarasashealingarts@gmail.com

7759 Herschel Ave. Unit B
La Jolla, CA 92037

Robert Sidell

Robert Sidell is the author of The Gateway, Discover the Power to create an Outrageously Prosperous and Happy life. He hosts The Gateway Show on AM 840 KXNT, which is the number 1 talk radio station in Las Vegas. Robert has been an attorney for 41 years, and is a member of the California, Nevada and Arizona bar associations.

Faith

Faith is the substance of things hoped for, the evidence of things unseen!

Contact Robert Sidell, Esq.

3415 West Charleston Blvd
Las Vegas, NV 89102

rbsidell@gmail.com

RobertSidell.com

dreampowershow.com

Suzy Prudden

Internationally acclaimed speaker and seminar leader, author, fitness expert, master hypnotherapist, body/mind pioneer, success and mindset coach and book publisher. You've seen her on Oprah, The Today Show and Good Morning America. The New York Times says, "If Suzy is talking about it today, the rest of the country will be talking about it tomorrow."

Fame

A position of responsibility to make the world a better place.

Contact Suzy Prudden

310-640-8885

suzyprudden@gmail.com

ittybittypublishing.com

suzyprudden.com

311 Main St., Suite D
El Segundo, CA 90245

Chellie Campbell

Chellie Campbell, author of *The Wealthy Spirit, Zero to Zillionaire, From Worry to Wealthy* published in 7 countries and 6 languages, has been treating Money Disorders - Spending Bulimia and Income Anorexia in her Financial Stress Reduction® Workshops for over 25 years. She is widely quoted in major media including *Redbook, Good housekeeping* and more than 50 popular books. Chellie.com

Fantabulous

What comes out when trying to say fantastic and fabulous at the same time.

Contact Chellie Campbell

www.chellie.com

Suzzy Canny

I was born a baby boomer, married and had three beautiful children and four grandchildren.   I am married to the love of my life and second husband Thomas Canny. I have had several careers, all the while sewing for others gave me my greatest joy. In 2014 I turned the joy of sewing into a business.

Fashion

A tool to express the essence of an individual's style.

Contact Suzzy Canny

Suzzy Canny, Custom Seamstress

http://www.suzzycanny.com/

Phone: 818 984-3287

Email: suzzycanny@sbcglobal.net

Lori Zapata

As Best Selling Author of "Women Who Rock" and "Rock Your Life", Lori discovered healing through writing. Her photography has been seen in The Chicago Tribune, New York Hockey Journal, Linda Eder's CDs, and other publications. Being Mom to two amazing young men is her greatest joy. Contact and/or View Lori's photography at <u>LoriZapata.com</u>.

Fearless

Not a Life without Fear, but Boldly
Facing Fear Head On, to Live Your
Dreams!

Contact Lori Zapata

www.LoriZapata.com

info@LoriZapata.com

P.K. Odle

P.K. Odle is a Master Feng Shui Consultant and Executive Director of the renowned *American Feng Shui Institute*®, where she's taught since 1998. Her consultations and revolutionary 'Personal Directions Self-Mastery Toolbox' teaches clients how manage their unique 15° Magnetic Directions that affect their entire life. She privately evaluates/consults on existing structures and project development for residential and commercial clients worldwide.

Feng Shui

A centuries-old Chinese system of optimizing your environment to support your wellbeing, relationships and prosperity.

Contact P.K. Odle

The Feng Shui Advantage[®]

626-288-1669

www.PKFengShui.com

PK@PKFengShui.com

Annette McCullough

Annette McCullough started her financial career in the early 70's with real estate investment. She then moved into finance. As a Real Estate Broker, licensed Mortgage Broker, Insurance Agent, business owner and Financial Advisor and Coach, she has helped thousands of people understand and learn to manage their finances. She is very active educating and assisting people to gain control of their financial world.

Finance

The control and management of the flow of money in all areas of life.

Contact Annette McCullough, PhD

626-399-7110

Annette.Money@gmail.com

Joana Brown

Board Certified Massage Therapist & Health Instructor. #1 International Best Selling Author speaker. Corporate Rehabilitation Specialist, worked with Chris Kingsley and American Hockey league minor league for the NHL - LA Kings & New York Islanders, Ongoing Consultant with Marriott Hotels and Scripps Hospitals.

Fitness

I was born unable to walk till age 8 -
FITNESS became my number 1 priority.

Contact Joana Brown

Sit Be Fit

http://sitbefit.co/

619-981-2852

Ross Wright

Ross Wright AKA Elvis Schoenberg; A modern
day renaissance man, or schizophrenic
depending on whom you ask; A professional:
composer, arranger, conductor, band-leader,
musician, radio personality, film producer,
bestselling author, entrepreneur, real estate
investor, speaker, and fitness instructor.
Ross lives in Los Angles where he fronts and
conducts his 30 piece musical ensemble "The
Orchestre Surreal."

Floccinaucinihilpilification

To describe or regard something as
unimportant, of having no value, or
being worthless.

Contact Ross Wright

www.theorchestresurreal.com

Osurreal@sbcglobal.net

Cindy Isaacson

Cindy Isaacson is Concert Coordinator for Good For The Soul Music and spiritual retreat facilitator using sacred scripture, music, poetry, and contemplative practices to refresh and nourish your soul.

Forgiveness

A grace filled awakening of letting go and giving over to receive life anew.

Contact Cindy Isaacson

cindyisaacson@yahoo.com

Rosie Aiello

After a 23 year marriage, Rosie Aiello, MBA engineered an international escape from the Middle East to save her daughter and herself from domestic violence. Stunned by PTSD and nearly mentally destroyed, she reinvented herself since arriving back in the United States, started her own business, and became a speaker, best-selling author and an international awarding-winning entrepreneur.

Freedom

Everyday looking out my window in San Diego since my international escape from domestic violence.

Contact Rosie Aiello

www.theloveiskindnetwork.com

Andrea Geisinger

Andrea Geisinger is a teacher and healer at heart. She has been working on her own personal development for over two decades, starting out how to become a better parent and ultimately discovering who she truly is and connecting to her own power.

Andrea inspires people and empowers you to follow your heart and go for what you truly want.

Fun

Fun makes me feel alive! Fun is the zest of my life!

Contact Andrea Geisinger

415-613-0140

andrea.geisinger@gmail.com

your-healing-journey.com

TK O'Geary

TK O'Geary, is a TED speaker coach, certified World Class Speaking coach, and an in-demand speaker coach. She helps geeks (in any genre, topic, or organization) learn how to better communicate (in meetings, speaking to an audience, or on the phone). Not to turn geeks into professional speakers, but to turn geeks into those who can be understood.

Geek

Someone who is extremely enthusiastic, experienced, and/or knowledgeable about a subject.

Contact TK O'Geary

TheGeekWhoCanSpeak@gmail.com

G

Lisa Brumm

A comprehensive financial services firm focusing on women and women-owned businesses. We spark financial curiosity in a non-planning fee based model and independently broker to all income levels. We foster a shame-free zone and collaborate with clients to help them achieve financial organization, efficiency and prosperity. Alleviate money stress, anxiety and our clients repeatedly say we help them sleep better at night!

Girlfriend

A female friend/confidant. A Financial Advisor/Planner; your Financial Professional who's got your back!

Contact Lisa Brumm

MY FINANCIAL GIRLFRIEND
1455 NW Irving Street, Suite 200
Portland OR 97209

o) 971-232-5831
c) 503-890-0276

lisa@myfinancialgirlfriend.com

www.facebook.com/myfinancialgf/

www.linkedin.com/in/lisabrumm

Genevieve Mitchell

Genevieve Mitchell is an owner and partner at Goddess Ink. She is committed to a world of economic justice, environment sustainability and respect for humans and other members of our earth community. She is a Priestess, a socially responsible investor, a photo artist, a mother and grandmother of three. She enjoys live music, good books and interesting people.

Goddess

The essence of the Sacred feminine. The Great Goddess, Mother Nature, the Great Mother, Creatrix.

Contact Genevieve Mitchell

www.goddess-ink.com

Christine Blosdale

Award-winning Radio Personality and Host of the "Out of The Box With Christine" Podcast Show, Author, Motivational Speaker and Consultant for Authors, Entertainers and Entrepreneurs. Specializing in the skilled field of Interviews, Infotainment and Infomercials, Christine has also raised well over Sixteen Million Dollars for both Non Profits and Private Companies.

Goosebumps

The tingly feeling you get throughout your body when something spectacular is about to happen.

Contact Christine Blosdale

www.ChristineBlosdale.com

OutOfTheBoxWithChristine@gmail.com

Podcast: OutOfTheBoxWithChristine.com

G

Katherin Scott

Katherin Scott is affectionately named "Coach Cupid" by the media and many of her now blissfully married clients. Their happily-ever-after stories are proof positive of the impact Katherin's time-tested methods deliver for those who are ready for love now.

Gracious

Compassionate, courteous, elegant, loving, kind, charming, accepting, tactful, calm, comforting, generous, holding space for others.

Contact Katherin Scott

www.KatherinScott.com

KatherinScott@yahoo.com

G

Cathie Peterson

I am a wife and mother of two adult children. I have my own relationship marketing business and I spend my days sending out gratitude and kindness. It is the best job in the world!

Gratitude

The magical ingredient in life that makes people know they matter.

Contact Cathie Peterson

WeSendBrownies@gmail.com

www.sendoutcards.com/bestcardsoc

714-335-7308

G

Patty Hedrick, RN

RN Healthcare Consultant with 30 years experience navigating through the healthcare system, helping others achieve their highest level of independence by offering support, guidance and resources. She enjoys working as a Nurse Entrepreneur, speaking, traveling and spending time with family and friends.

Gumption

Determination, courageous and resourceful. A word I aspire to live up to.

Contact Patty Hedrick, RN

MLHCC Inc. Healthcare Consultants
222 N. Pacific Coast Highway Suite 2000
El Segundo, CA 90245

Office: 310-335-2005

Cell: 310-962-7502

Fax: 877-240-9519

Email: pattyh@mlhcc.com

Website: www.mlhcc.com

G

Sonia Shafazand

A young single mother, and immigrant; Sonia
admits to having lots of anxiety at that time and
attributes it to being responsible for two
toddlers' life, alone and in a new country. Focus
on what mattered most and personal growth
were the path she chose courageously. She
earned her Masters and now works with
executives, professionals, the self-employed,
stay at home moms and students.

Happiness

The everlasting flow of joy stemming from seeds of gratitude, love and accepting what is.

Contact Sonia Shafazand

Trusted Advisor, Life Coach & Mentor to those who choose to have a Better, Happier Life NOW.

Email: sonia@Shafazand.com

Website: BandOfCourage.com

Phone: 408-605-9694

Rita Dandorf

Rita Dandorf is a Licensed Massage Therapist, who has owned and operated Healing Dynamics Massage, LLC in Scottsdale, AZ since 1994. Rita empowers her clients through a holistic healing system by working with the five elements, allowing the soul to spring forth, elevating their consciousness while revitalizing their bodies so they can enjoy a harmonious and vibrant life.

Harmony

Harmony is a noun. Harmony is agreement, accord, cooperation, understanding, friendship, fellowship, peacefulness and oneness.

Contact Rita Dandorf

www.healingdynamicsmassage.com

Phone - 480 729 6282 ext 606

rita@healingdynamicsmassage.com

Elizabeth Weiner

Elizabeth A. Weiner, MS, CBP is a holistic
practitioner who believes healing is possible.
She is passionate about creating better health
naturally. Liz partners with her clients to heal
their minds and bodies with a focus on mental
wellness and pain relief. Her go-to modality is
BodyTalk, which reminds the body how to heal
itself.

Healing

Restoring health by repairing, resetting and rebalancing; becoming well, whole and healthy.

Contact Elizabeth Weiner

www.elizabethweiner.com

949-864-6900

liz@perspectivehw.com

Bonnie Perkins

Bonnie Perkins - here is my secret "Only the Heart can see and feel clearly the truth of living abundantly with purpose and vision attracting light-minded people to do the same living with Devine Purpose Heart2Heart.

Heart

I live life to the fullness from living
successful to purposeful driven by Heart.

Contact Bonnie Perkins

www.bonnieperkins.com

Angela Hall

I love discovering new ways to accomplish my goals on my websites and sharing that knowledge with others. My approach to teaching is simplistic and easy for anyone to follow, even if you have never seen a dashboard (except maybe in your car!).

Helpful

A willingness to give assistance to someone, adding value to their life or business.

Contact Angela Hall

https://thathelpfulchick.com/

502-216-0996

ajhall2012@gmail.com

J.V. Crum III

JV Crum III, MBA, JD, MS, is a serial-entrepreneur, best-selling author, high performance coach, speaker, and Host of Conscious Millionaire Podcast, which Inc Magazine named a Top 13 Business Podcast. He coaches business owners and business coaches to achieve their First Million. JV also provides masterminds, trainings, and group programs for conscious entrepreneurs through his Conscious Millionaire Institute, LLC.

High-Performance

A commitment to upscale your results by consistently achieving your personal best.

Contact J.V. Crum III,

www.ConsciousMillionaire.com

jvcrum3@ConsciousMillionaire.com

Tressa Pope

Tressa Pope is a Licensed Mortgage Loan Consultant, specializing in helping people buy their first home. She has been nicknamed, "The Holistic Lender" because of the way she educates & guides her clients through the home loan process.

Home

Much more than just a house; a place to feel safe, secure and loved.

Contact Tressa Pope,

www.tressapope.com

Direct: 818-422-6083

Email: tressa@tressapope.com

Gale Barbe

Gale Barbe is a dedicated mother, housewife, and empty nester. She is certified as a master practitioner of NLP (Neuro Linguistic Programming), hypnotherapy, time techniques, EFT (Emotional Freedom Techniques), success coaching and Reiki Practitioner. She is passionate about helping other empty nesters with their health and happiness by using these tools and other natural and holistic practices.

Hope

It's the anchor of the soul where courage, confidence, and happiness emerge for your purpose.

Contact Gale Barbe

www.galebarbe.com

galebarbe@gmail.com

626-905-5240

Judy Schriener

Judy Schriener is a longtime journalist, author and radio show host – "Off the Record with Judy" on Star Worldwide Networks – who gives people an inside look into the lives and mindsets of successful people. She is a newshound and a Denver Broncos fan, and she lives for worldwide travel.

Humor

Appreciation of absurd, funny or amusing situations; valuable aid in getting through life.

Contact Judy Schriener

judywriter@gmail.com

http://www.offtherecordwithjudy.com

PO Box 12052,
Chandler, AZ 85248

Lancing Kreple

Lance Kreple is a junior in high school. He is a second degree black belt in TaeKwanDo and former child actor. He is a varsity Volleyball player and a student of acrobatics and Parcore.

Hyperbole

Most of the girls in my class talk in hyperbole.

Contact Lancing Kreple

lancingkreple@icloud.com

Melody Keymer Harper

Melody Keymer Harper, speaker, bestselling author, entertainer, and Radio/TV Host, has shared the stage and screen with celebrities **Elvis Presley**, **Johnny Carson**, **Elizabeth Taylor** and speaking giants: **Brian Tracy**, **Les Brown**, and **Jack Canfield**. Over 40 years experience teaching, speaking and communication skills to stand out as a Celebrity in your industry, get more clients, and make more money.

Ignite

Set a spark of immense intensity and passion from your message that spreads like wildfire.

Contact Melody Keymer Harper

www.IgniteYourSpeakingPower.com

melody@IgniteYourSpeakingPower.com

949-400-8111

Lynn Swearingen

Lynn Swearingen is a Consulting Hypnotist (CH) and Certified Instructor (CI), molding the next wave of science-based, transformative hypnotists.

Lynn is a HypnoCoach®, Neuro-Linguistic Hypnotist and member of the National Federation of Neuro-Linguistic Programming and National Guild of Hypnotists.

A true Hypno-preneur, her effective, no-nonsense life-coaching harnesses the power of the subconscious for turbo-charged success, shattering self-limiting beliefs and blocks.

Imagine

Our infinitely creative minds find expression in IMAGINATION, where the impossible meets limitless possibility.

Contact Lynn Swearingen

Url: www.bayareahypnotherapy.com

Tel: 415-923-7611

Email: info@bayareahypnotherapy.com

Debbie Downie

Debbie Downie is an Image Impact Strategist revealing your God-given beauty with your best looks via color and silhouettes. The right colors make your skin glow and your eyes pop, while wearing the right clothing for your shape draws attention to your best body features. Let Debbie Downie lift up your smile, finding your perfect look and style.

Impact

To create a strikingly, unforgettable presence via clothing, grooming and persona optimizing the best you.

Contact Debbie Downie

www.debbiedownieenterprises.com

732-245-7589

debbiedownie@comcast.net

Cathie-Ann Lippman, MD

Dr. Cathie-Ann Lippman is an Environmental and Preventive Medicine MD in Beverly Hills. She's an expert on nutrition, allergies, sensitivities and imbalances. Dr. Lippman is also an expert on how chemicals in our air, foods and homes affect our health. She has been an advocate for natural health for over 30 years and has been referenced in Suzanne Somers' books *Ageless*, *Breakthrough* and *Knockout*.

Inflammation

Our body's self-protective acute and/or chronic response to a physical and/or emotional distress.

Contact Dr. Lippman

www.cathielippmanmd.com

291 S. La Cienega Blvd., Suite 409, Beverly Hills, CA 90211

310-289-8430

email: doclipp@gmail.com

Michelle Calloway

<u>Michelle Calloway</u> is a Speaker, Int'l Bestselling
Author, and the Founder and CEO of
<u>REVEALiO, Inc.</u>, an augmented reality (AR)
video marketing company. Her goal is to make
these AR interactive experiences accessible and
affordable for everyone, to enhance human
relationships, and empower business owners to
have more impact, influence, and income.

Innovative

To use creative thinking to generate new useful purposes for existing concepts and inventions

Contact Michelle Calloway

https://revealio.com

415-870-7894

mcalloway@revealio.com

Patti Smith

Patti Smith is a certified Life Success Coach and Speaker. For most of her adult life Patti has studied success principles, giving her valuable insight and the ability to have successfully achieved her dreams both professionally and personally. The deep personal impact of losing her sister to cancer inspired Patti to follow her passion, helping people connect with their inner joy and purpose!

Inspire

To spark creative imagination by igniting the soul, rousing the power to influence and impact.

Contact Patti Smith

Patti Smith Innovative Coaching, LLC

Email: Patti@PattiSmithCoaching.com

Cell: 213-422-5596

www.PattiSmithCoaching.com

Judy Hersch

Judy, a certified Master Life & Business Coach, is the founder of Evolution Solutions, and a Professional Speaker, Corporate Trainer and Workshop Leader.

Judy has coached and trained organizations, groups, and individuals in the U.S. and abroad for 20 years, helping audiences and clients discover and achieve extraordinary success in the areas of health and well-being, relationships, career, and time and money freedom.

InspirActional

Inspiring others to take meaningful action, especially something creative or spiritual.

Contact Judy Hersch

Master Life and Business Coach

310-802-9336

Evolution Solutions, LLC

www.myevolutionsolutions.com

J

Pat Price

My devotion to clients comes from my own experience, becoming responsible for my toddler brother and my teenaged self when mom died. Lack of coverage left us vulnerable and took away many opportunities. My mission is to provide supplemental benefits that help business owners protect their employees from the indirect costs of being injured or sick. Contact me at BenefitsByPrice.com

Insurance

When you are faced with extraordinary circumstances, supplemental insurance can help pay your everyday expenses.

Contact Pat Price

Benefits by Price

Cell: 954-614-2900

Fax: 954-564-3179

Insurance@patprice.net

BenefitsByPrice.com

Toni Caruso

Toni Caruso has over 30 years of event experience in the entertainment, corporate and entrepreneurial worlds. Her mission is to produce **Signature Events** that are exciting, engaging, unique and informative. Where business professionals can connect & collaborate. Your guests walk in with a dream and leave with the tools to make that dream it a reality. She is a RockStar!

Integrity

The quality of being honest and fair.
Doing what you say you will do.

Contact Toni Caruso

Event Producer

CarusoSignatureEvents.com

Toni@carusosignatureevents.com

818-800-0752

Michele Mariscal

Michele Mariscal, owner of EnergyM, is a speaker and skilled facilitator and coach. She combines her background in health, wellness, and spiritual healing to help individuals find greater meaning in life through heart intelligence. Her specialty is helping people move through grief.

Intelligence

Informed knowing woven together from inner and outer sources.

Contact Michele Mariscal

www.EnergyM.org

916-402-6188

info@EnergyM.org

Roland Takaoka

In Memoriam

Roland Takaoka, Founder/President of MINMAX Media, was a talented internet marketing expert, beloved by people worldwide. Despite being paralyzed after his third stroke, Roland's moto was "Expand in Joy." Media host of The Monday Morning Marketing Smarties Show. Co-host of Stroke TV with Aaron Avila. Consultant on The Difference Makers. His legacy continues through his book, "Adventures In Rehab, Inspired By A Stroke."

Intend

"An action you take to bring about a desired outcome."

Roland Takaoka

1953 ~ 2018

You will be missed...
...but never forgotten

Rick Bloom

Rick Bloom is an entrepreneur based in Ojai, California.

He has been most productive running his own businesses since the early 80's. More recently, Rick and his wife, Debe, are living the life of their dreams, traveling North American in their RV, meeting new people and sharing their passion for a healthy life and multiple streams of passive income.

Intentional

To take planned, purposeful actions toward completion of a task or achieving a goal.

Contact Rick Bloom

415-716-6637

http://DebeAndRick.com

rick@DebeAndRick.com

J

Peter Rozsa

I first started to wake up during the Kennedy-King period of the 1960s. It made me want to make the world work better. Since then, I mostly try to envision how this might happen.

My words are not true neologisms.
They are outgrowths of The Golden Rule.

Inter-augmenting

To augment means to add on or improve.
Inter implies within a group or system.

Contact Peter Rozsa

peterozsa@sbcglobal.net

Jonathan Flier

Jonathan Flier, Licensed Marriage and Family
Therapist creates emotionally safe, empathic
connections with clients. He specializes in
working with men, treating trauma, anxiety, high
conflict and passionless couples. Jonathan
guides individuals and couples in creating strong
bonds of intimacy for satisfying and enduring
relationships. He helps clients recover from
traumatic experiences utilizing somatic
treatments such as EMDR and the Trauma
Resiliency Model.

Intimacy

An experience of closeness in a context of emotional and physical safety.

Contact Jonathan Flier

Phone: 310-552-5338

Website: https://jonathanflier.com

Email: jonathan@jonathanflier.com

CeCe Converse, CPCC

CeCe Converse is a Coach and Intuitive helping women thrive after trauma. Her own experience with sexual abuse and recovery inspired her to become a Certified Credentialed Coach. Since 2003 she has helped hundreds of women re-create successful lives, relationships and businesses. Ready to step into more love, ease, money, balance and joy? Call CeCe to start "Thriving After Trauma".

Intuition

"In to it-ability": using our vast senses to know, see, feel, or hear spirit guidance.

Contact CeCe Converse, CPCC

www.cececonverse.com

415-885-9700

cece@cececonverse.com

Mark McCulloch

Ancient Crest

Pet healer, Life Activations, Pet Whisperer;
All creatures, great and small.
No pet too small, No pet too large.

Invictus

Invincible, Unconquered, Unsubdued,
Undisputed, Undefeated.

Contact Mark McCulloch

lisamed8r@gmail.com

Linda McCarthy

Linda McCarthy is a Franchise Owner for **Business Network Int'l-BNI** of Ventura County, California. BNI provides a positive, supportive, and structured program for quality business referrals.

Linda is a contributing author in 2 books, "Masters of Success" and "Masters of Sales", both by Dr. Ivan Misner and Don Morgan. Best Sellers for the New York Times and Wall Street Journal.

Joy

Happy is a condition of our circumstances and Joy is a condition of our heart.

Contact Linda McCarthy

Executive Director
BNI of Ventura County, CA, USA

805-850-0157 (office)

www.bni-vc.com

http://www.facebook.com/bniventura

Y

Katrina Sawa

Katrina Sawa is an energetic, tell-it-like-it-is speaker, award-winning "JumpStart Your Biz Coach", Creator of the Jumpstart Your Marketing® System and Author of Love Yourself Successful, Jumpstart Your New Business Now and the Jumpstart Your _____ Compilation book. She helps entrepreneurs turn their inspiration and ideas into smooth-running, consistently profitable businesses FAST. Grab some of her free trainings online at www.JumpstartYourMarketing.com.

Jumpstart

Giving someone a boost, rejuvenating their confidence and/or motivating them into forward, practical, purposeful action.

Contact Katrina Sawa

916-872-4000

www.JumpstartYourMarketing.com

katrina@jumpstartyourmarketing.com

Egle and Roger Dumadag

Egle & Roger Dumadag represent Enagic, the Japanese company which makes the **Kangen Water® System** producing alkaline, antioxidant, super hydrating **Kangen Water®.** They offer a **FREE 2 week trial of the Kangen Water® System** to use in your home or business! Save money and help reduce plastic in our environment by drinking Kangen water and become healthier all at the same time!

Kangen

Return to origin (in Japanese) alkaline, antioxidant, superhydrating water used for drinking, cooking, beauty & cleaning.

Contact Egle and Roger Dumadag

www.Demo.Aquamazing.com

646-247-3529 Roger/646-831-8841 Egle

info@Aquamazing.com

Aquamazing Facebook
Aquamazing Instagram
Aquamazing YouTube

Sita Fischer

Sita Fischer is an Artist, Designer, Entrepreneur, Health and Wellness Expert, Changing lives with Ketones and Electrically Reduced Antioxidant Water.

Ketones

Lifting the cerebral curtain with
unreckoned performance…
The metabolic white knight rises…
Burn Fat Burn!

Contact Sita Fischer

CEO, Equiroc

775-235-2255

www.sita.drinkyoursample.com
www.kangenrejuvenation.com
www.sitafischer.com
www.stufft.com

Debbie Mrazek

Debbie Mrazek is president of The Sales Company, a Texas-based firm that helps hundreds of entrepreneurs, individuals, and corporations better assess, understand and engage in practical purposeful selling. She is a high energy, get it done sooner than later, kick butt and take names Sales Coach, Consultant, Trainer, Speaker and Author. Kindness is at the core of ALL of her success! www.The-Sales-Company.com

Kindness

Kindness is a super power that PAYS in business and life.

Contact Debbie Mrazek

www.The-Sales-Company.com

214-676-8486

Debbie@The-Sales-Company.com

Katie Sevenants

Since 2002, Katie has worked as a Certified Elite MUA and Independent Distributor with SeneGence International, one of the fastest growing skincare and cosmetic companies. Katie educates and empowers women while giving them the tools to look BEAUTIFUL, feel CONFIDENT and become FINANCIALLY FREE!

Kiss

A passionate moment that ignites a feeling of fresh, youthful confidence!

Contact Katie Sevenants

www.KissMeKatie411.com

425-231-2282

Katie@KissMeKatie411.com

Kimberly Carter

A business owner with a demonstrated history of working in the insurance industry since 1993. Skilled in Commercial Property & Casualty, Excess & Surplus Lines, Homeowners Associations, Workers' Compensation, Cyber Liability and Personal Lines.

Kite

Freedom to fly up high in the breeze surrounded by endless color.

Contact Kimberly Carter

Framers' Insurance Agency Owner

Office: 818-914-4304
Cell: 818-521-5644
Fax: 818-854-7334

kcarter1@farmersagent.com

License 0B75891

Dame Kim Conrad, M.A.

Dame Kim Conrad is an award-winning, internationally known global leader, consultant, corporate speaker and engaging facilitator. Her artistic life's work is part of the archives at the National Museum of Women in the Arts in Washington, D.C. In 2018, the special honor of knighthood was bestowed upon Dame Kim Conrad by The Order of St. John Russian Grand Priory (OOSJ).

Languaginations

A play-filled partnership with language that instills and ignites the imagination!

Contact Dame Kim Conrad

www.KimConrad.com

Facebook:
www.facebook.com/kimconradvisionary

303-439-0261

kim@kimconrad.com

Wanda Toro Turini

Wanda is the founder of Ketch. Combining innovative tech with killer strategy, Wanda pioneered the premier lead generation program for keynote speakers, business development executives and entrepreneurs who speak to share their brilliance and collect leads.
Text LEAD to 411321 to receive her brief on the 4 killer strategies that can transform your talk into a lead generating machine.

Lead

A business prospect who has a defined problem for which you have a defined solution.

Contact Wanda Toro Turini, Pharm D

President of ecoFiles, Inventor of Ketch

Email: wanda@ecoFilesMobile.com

Phone: 908-603-5401

Website: Ketchword.com

Ketchword: Text LEAD to 411321

$\mathcal{L}$

Dr. Emily LeTran

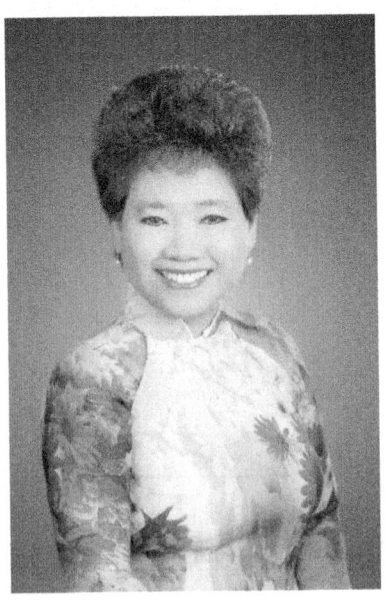

Dr. Emily Letran came to the US as a refugee and excelled as CEO of multiple dental offices. As a high performance coach, she creatively balances work and life with 3 children, dedicated to helping business professionals maximize their potential, stream line business and increase profits. Her clients gain more clarity, become highly productive, and position themselves as influencers to create more impact.

Leverage

Maximize one's ability & capacity using other's expertise, manpower, resource , and connection, achieving greater results.

Contact Dr. Emily Letran

emily@exceptionalleverage.com

www.DrEmilyLetran.com

626-808-5762

Dame Shellie Hunt

Founder of Success is By Design & The Women of Global Change. Shellie's gift of transformational impact has taken clients beyond motivation, to lasting results! Shellie is described in the international press as "One of the best orators & coaches of human potential available for public speaking and a master of business structure and multiple sources of income."

Light

Something that makes vision possible! A beacon to illuminate enlightenment!

Contact Dame Shellie Hunt

Founder/CEO

Www.SuccessisbyDesign.com

Www.WomenofGlobalChange.com

Barbara Cunningham

Owner of Loyalty Processing where we help merchants reduce the fees, fears and frustrations of credit card processing. We'll do a free side by side analysis of your current statement and show you an 8% to 30% savings. I'm an ETA CPP, a Certified Payments Professional with over 15 years experience.

Loyalty

You're either 100% loyal or you're not loyal at all.

Contact Barbara Cunningham

Phone: 213-248-6787

E-Mail: Barbara@LoyaltyProcessing.com

www.loyaltyprocessing.com

Donna Burke

Donna has been a jack of all trades, she has
worked in aerospace, early intervention,
catering, film and theater, and publishing. She's
been a Certified Master Hypnotherapist and
Empowerment and Accountability Coach. She
has a BS in Marketing and holds the designation
of Certified Manager from the Institute of
Certified Professional Managers. Donna loves
all animals, especially her sweet little poodle.

Magic

That which happens spontaneously as a gift from the universe. Face to the left, Magical!

Contact Donna Burke

dlhb97@yahoo.com

$\mathcal{M}$

Marla Brucker

As a Peak Performance Coach, motivational
trainer and seminar leader, Marla has inspired
thousands worldwide conducting seminars and
training's in Energy Medicine and Psychokinesis
(spoon bending).   Marla has her Doctorate in
Clinical Hypnotherapy, is a Registered Hypnotic
Anesthesiologist, Master Practitioner of NLP,
certified in Energy Psychology and as a Laugh
leader. Marla is the CEO of the Motivational
Institute of Hypnotherapy.

Magnificence

Become *one* with your journey into your *magnificence.*

Contact Marla Brucker, DHC, R.HA

Motivational Institute of Hypnosis

858-587-0422

Marla@SanDiegoHypnosis.com

www.SanDiegoHypnosis.com

$\mathcal{M}$

Daniel Olexa

Daniel Olexa is the co-author of two Amazon #1 Bestsellers: *Practical Manifesting* and *A Pessimist's Guide to Manifesting.*

He has been recognized by Feedspot.com as one of the Top 100 Hypnotherapy Blogs in the world and was voted the Favorite Hypnotherapist and Life Coach in the South Bay (Los Angeles) area in 2018.

Manifest

To make the non-physical, physical. To bring an idea into reality. Thought becomes form.

Contact Daniel Olexa

www.danielolexa.com

daniel@danielolexa.com

310-746-5929

$\mathcal{M}$

Stephanie B. Stern

Stephanie B. Stern is an anomalous American Writer living in Los Angeles, CA with her husband, two adorable rescue cats and (hopefully one day soon) a very cute dog. Her interests are finding the 'middle c' key on the piano, trying to sing on tune, dabbling in screenwriting/producing, staying as healthy as can be done and Real Estate Investments.

Mendacity

Untruthful. A favorite Play, "Cat On a Hot Tin Roof" used the word beautifully.

Contact Stephanie B. Stern

www.passingyourrealestateexam.com

$\mathcal{M}$

George Partsalidis

George was born in Germany, grew up in Greece and he lives happily with his family in Toronto, Canada. He is a successful entrepreneur and real estate investor. George enjoys spreading his knowledge of business and life success. His goal is to teach his children by example, to love life, to conquer their fears and to CREATE their FUTURE.

Meraki

The soul, creativity, love, the essence of yourself put into your work or anything you do.

Contact George Partsalidis

www.georgepartsalidis.com

partsalidis@live.com

$\mathcal{M}$

Bonnie Patterino

Bonnie has been a Life Transformation Leader for over thirty years, helping thousands attain vitality and well-being.

She is a Wellness Spa Owner, #1 International Best Selling Author, and IIHA Certified Hand Print Analyst who decodes Soul Purpose. She teaches her GPS Your Path™ Metamorphosis Methods to help individuals and audiences find self-worth and an enlightened path to joy.

Metamorphosis

Crawl. Gorge to grow. Cocoon to digest limited self. Become higher self. Spread wings. FLY!

Contact Bonnie Patterino

website: www.gpsyourpath.com

office: 301-515-0470

email: gpsyourpath@gmail.com

Janie Becker, CMT

Janie Becker focuses on listening to caregivers' needs and helping them heal their physical and emotional traumas using aromatherapy and massage techniques. She is active in the community volunteering to support cancer research and childrens' charities. Contact her to subscribe to the monthly Caregivers Corner newsletter to get your free e-book for caregiver strategies at www.lessbrainstressnow.com.

Mindfulness

Conscious awareness on your purpose for the present moment.

Contact Janie Becker, the Encourager

Website: www.lessbrainstressnow.com

Email: aromatherapyplus@verizon.net

Phone: 562-728-8178   M-F 8-6 pst

Candace Burton

Master Life Coach, B.E.S.T. Elite Master, CCH Hypnotherapy, CMT Massage Therapy, Law of Attraction and Passion Test Facilitator, Rapid Resolution Therapy Facilitator, The Reconnection Facilitator, Burton Mindpower Release, Motivational Speaker, Telesessions, Best Selling Author.

Mindpower

Using the mind intending a chosen result while changing subconscious programs or beliefs if necessary.

Contact Candace Burton

DrCandaceBurton.com

954-993-3358

drcandaceburton@yahoo.com

Dale Ann Springer

Dale Ann Springer uses her 30+ years of Silicon Valley experience to address today's most crucial health issues with drug free leading-edge technology systems, targeting aliments such as stress, pain and sleeplessness.

Mindset

A positive mindset is essential in delivering positive results.

Contact Dale Ann Springer

www.newreality.com

916-806-7559

dale@newreality.com

Karen Worstell

Karen Worstell is CEO of Denver-based W Risk
Group who helps accelerate the career path of
women in Tech.. "When Tech women are
comfortable in their personal power, have clarity
on who they serve and the problem they'll solve,
and operate from the center of their leadership
abilities, they are unstoppable."

Mojo

That attribute that draws people to you so you excel in reaching your goals.

Contact Karen Worstell

PHONE:720-638-2646

FAX: 720-638-5959

WEB: www.karenworstell.com
        Karenworstell.com/mojo-maker

EMAIL: karen@wriskgroupllc.com

LinkedIn: http://www.linkedin.com/in/kar
enworstell

$\mathcal{M}$

Pamela Plick

Known as the "Money Mentor for Women,"
Pamela Plick believes strongly in educating and
empowering women to take control of their
financial future. Pamela is a CERTIFIED
FINANCIAL PLANNER™ practitioner
and Certified Money Coach (CMC)®, She's
founder and CEO of Pamela Plick Wealth
Management, LLC a fee-only Registered
Investment Advisory firm based in Palm Desert,
CA.

Money

Money is….
A powerful tool; To be used wisely;
To be respected; To be protected.

Contact Pamela Plick

www.pamelaplick.com

$\mathcal{M}$

Tamar Hermes

Tamar Hermes, The Wealth Warrior, helps women entrepreneurs make and keep more money. Her passion is coaching women to overcome emotional and practical barriers around their finances. She works to ensure that her clients feel empowered to earn as much as they want and to reach their financial goals.

Monetize

Make and keep more money for a lifetime.

Contact Tamar Hermes

www.tamarhermesinternational.com

818-857-6162

hello@tamarhermesinternational.com

$\mathcal{M}$

Laurel Rutledge

Laurel Rutledge is a senior HR Executive, Consultant, strategist and career transformation expert. Her global experience in risk management, strategic HR, audit and business enable her to help you successfully navigate your environment to develop and meet individual and team strategies and goals.

Navigator

She sees the best path to the goal, plans viable alternative routes, guides masterfully.

Contact Laurel Rutledge

welcome@laurelrutledge.com

www.laurelrutledge.com

+1 713-303-7947

$\mathcal{N}$

Sharón Lynn Wyeth

Sharón Lynn Wyeth is recognized
internationally as a name expert as she can
determine one's strengths, challenges, and the
purpose of one's life by deciphering a person's
name. Sharón created Neimology® Science, the
study of the placement of the letters in a name,
after 18 years of research.

Neimology

The study of the placement of the letters in a name and what they reveal.

Contact Sharón Lynn Wyeth

210-355-6115

info@KnowTheName.com

www.KnowTheName.com

Peter Rozsa

    I first started to wake up during the Kennedy-King period of the 1960s. It made me want to make the world work better. Since then, I mostly try to envision how this might happen.
    My words are not true neologisms.
They are outgrowths of The Golden Rule.

Omni-beneficent

Omni meaning in all directions plus beneficent includes benevolent, charitable, altruistic, humanitarian, neighborly, public-spirited, philanthropic;

Contact Peter Rozsa

peterozsa@sbcglobal.net

Joan Meijer

Joan Meijer is a bestselling author, editor and publisher. She writes thrillers under the pen name John Russell, and is one of the owners of Itty Bitty Publishing.

Onomatopoeia

Words that sound like definitions – "Pop" or "Wind". I love the sound of this word.

Contact Joan Meijer

joanmeijer123@gmail.com

www.ittybittypublishing.com

310-640-8885

Grace Bermudes

Stop feeling overwhelmed!
Save time and welcome more productivity and enjoyment into your life. Grace's enthusiastic no nonsense approach to organizing is why clients nationally enjoy getting organized with her. Visit Grace's website or text her to find out how she can help you take the guesswork out of getting organized.

Organized

The nexus of space, purpose, and placement; creating calm, clarity, beauty, and productivity.

Contact Grace Bermudes

Professional Organizer

www.GraceBermudes.com

grace@checkitoffyourlistnow.com

408-202-4272 phone and text

Dr. Judy Cook

Find out more about Dr. Judy Cook at:

www.GoDrJudy.com

Outlook

What you focus on, good or bad, creates the Outlook and course of your life.

Contact Dr. Judy Cook

www.GoDrJudy.com

Tanya Brown

Tanya Brown is no stranger to adversity or trauma. With the loss of her sister, Nicole Brown Simpson, she has faced overwhelming life challenges but used these obstacles to ultimately improve the quality of her life. Today, she shares the tools to Find Peace Amid YOUR Daily Chaos. Tanya speaks and advocates for mental health and domestic violence issues.

Overcome

Delete the need to understand everything. We don't need to understand everything some things just are.

Contact Tanya Brown

http://www.tanyabrown.net

Phone: 949-278-5550

David Medansky

David Medansky, a retired divorce attorney, is an international best-selling author, and weight reduction specialist.

In July of 2016, his doctor told him to lose weight because he didn't want David dying of a heart attack.

Within four months, Medansky dropped 50 pounds. He wrote about his inspirational weight-reduction journey in his book, ***Discover Your Thinner Self***.

Overweight

Being *overweight* or fat is having more body fat than is optimally healthy.

Contact David Medansky

www.CreateYourThinnerSelf.com

Phone: 602-721-521

Email: davidmedansky@gmail.com

Corinne Enslin

Corinne Enslin was a leading designer in the
Pacific Design Center for 10 years and has
managed three Kitchen and Bath showrooms
on the West coast. She has been running her
own architectural interior design firm and
showroom for 22 years in Los Angeles, CA.
They specialize in High-end remodels and new
construction from planning to custom interior
procurement.

Passion

The deepest compelling desires and gifts within that radiate from your existence...

Contact Corinne Enslin

www.CorinneEnslin.com

www.interiordesignbusinessblueprint.com

818-919-0997 cell

310-954-0222 office

Design@CorinneEnslin.com

Dale Ann Springer

Dale Ann Springer uses her 30+ years of Silicon Valley experience to address today's most crucial health issues with drug free leading-edge technology systems, targeting aliments such as stress, pain and sleeplessness.

"I learned the word perfect from Suzy Prudden and it changed my life."

Perfect

Having the Mindset of seeing things as perfect will make it so.

Contact Dale Ann Springer

www.newreality.com

916-806-7559

dale@newreality.com

Gary Howarth

Find out more about Gary Howarth at:

www.vaxishub.com

Persistence

When you don't give up, you can have everything you want.

Contact Gary Howarth

www.vaxishub.com

Julie Anderson

Julie Anderson is an international public speaker; wielding her expertise in brain science to bring solution-based training into organizations and with entrepreneurs for business, communications, relationship and life success resulting in: increasing productivity, skyrocketing sales, preventing conflicts, and breaking through barriers in business and life. She uniquely blends science and psychology with humor and relatability to her clients.

Personality

The combination of DNA coding and life experience. The brain wiring that makes you, you.

Contact Julie "Brain Lady" Anderson

www.YourBestMindOnline.com

info@YourBestMindOnline.com

800-799-5877

Christine Lapidus

My clients build financial balance, protecting their families, and businesses from the many threats to their financial wellbeing. I help teach them to protect, save, invest and grow their resources so that they can have – "A Good Life, For the Rest of Your Life."

Playcheck

The "paycheck" that comes from a well-planned pension, annuity, or investment while in retirement.

Contact Christine Lapidus

christine_lapidus@pacificadvisors.com

818-920-8395

www.pacificadvisors.com/clapidus

Carolyn K. McGraw

Wellness Practitioner, Educational Consultant, Youth Life Coach, Poet, TV Host on "Life on Purpose" on <u>WBTVN.TV</u>. Master's degree, over 20 years teaching and 15 years as Hypnotherapist. Featured on TV talking about her At-Risk students using Poetry-Therapy. Uncover your "Happiness Blueprint" in her Coaching/Healing program.

Poetry

Life reflections, rhythmically, emotionally illuminating truth with wisdom flowing, soul melodies singing your HEALING remedy.

Contact Carolyn K. McGraw

carolynkmcgraw.com

inharmony11@gmail.com

916-844-6136

Laurel Rolls

Laurel INSPIRES her clients to discover their own POSSIBILITIES and pursue them NOW! Her strong intuition, insightfulness and CURIOSITY supports her clients in creating their own unique fabric of possibilities and creative actions. Laurel guides her clients through awareness of limiting beliefs and behaviors – the landmines keeping them from success and happiness –<u>and eliminate them</u>!

Possibilities

Possibilities are all around us...Use curiosity to acknowledge, embrace, explore and make them happen!

Contact Laurel Rolls

Laurel@LaurelRolls.com

www.TheConnectionLanguage.com

214-770-3854

Liz Lewinson

Award-winning author Liz Lewinson is a motivational speaker and longtime practitioner and teacher of meditation and mindfulness. *Women, Meditation, and Power* is her most recent book. She led film/television PR and marketing departments in Hollywood and owned a technology consulting firm on Wall Street. A former resident of New York, she now lives in Los Angeles.

Power

Power in nature is fluidity and change. Possessing life-delivering bodies, transformational leadership, women represent power.

Contact Liz Lewinson

www.lizlewinson.com

liz@lizlewinson.com

https://www.linkedin.com/in/lizllew/

Genevieve Burciaga, RN BSN

Genevieve Burciaga is a Registered Nurse who has a background in Holistic Lifestyle and Nutrition. She has graduated with her Bachelors in Nursing with an emphasis on Public Health and started her career straight into the aesthetic and wellness world. She combines the latest beauty treatments with evidence based nutrition protocols.

Pre-Tox

Lifestyle philosophy and strategic approach to preventive self healthjar care that ensures health and wellness.

Contact Genevieve Burciaga, RN BSN

Rnknows.com

Healthjar.com

213-925-5936

Rn@healthjar.com

Dani Zandel

Dani Zandel is a "Process Specialist".
She is the Award Winning Author of "How to
Create Customer Loyalty." Her experience stems
from 20 years in Auto Dealership
Communications Management and 6 years of
operating Mailbox Joy Marketing, an
independent representation of Send Out Cards,
Greeting Cards and Gifts. She lives in Los
Angeles, California with family. "Success is but
process."

Process

Consistent and repeated actions, often in sequential order, leading to a specific goal or outcome.

Contact Dani Zandel

310-428-3362

zandeldm@aol.com

Evelyn Siegel

Cash Flow Services works with new and existing businesses that would like to accept credit cards as a means of payment. If you have a current merchant account, we offer a free detailed analysis of your fees and rates.

I started Cash Flow Services in 1997, to help businesses of all sizes increase their sales and flexibility by accepting credit cards.

Profit

Profit is what we all want – sales, money, earnings, revenue, proceeds and income.

Contact Evelyn Siegel

www.cashflowservice.com

P: 310-826-4847

F: 310-820-3447

$\mathscr{P}$

Wendy Kashefi

Wendy is a psychic tarot card reader who inspires through her empathy, enthusiasm and sparkle, finds her work fascinating since every person is different and every reading is different. She encourages her clients to use information gained in her sessions to strategize choices, bearing in mind that the legacy of forgotten past situations may be provoking knee-jerk reactions in present time.

Psychic

Intuitive insights, layered with tarot techniques, are tools for brainstorming options in relationships, career, life.

Contact Wendy Kashefi

www.wendytarot.com

Wendy@wendytarot.com

Janel Prator

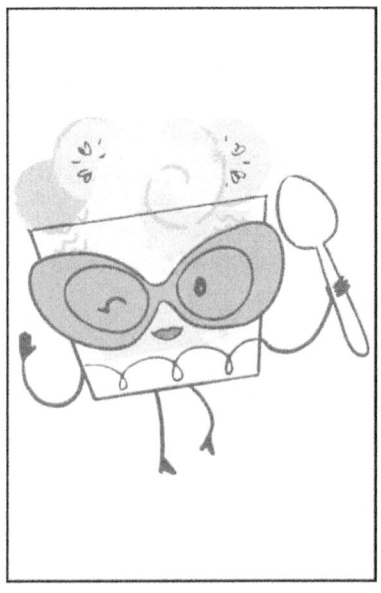

The Puddery, established in 2006, by Founder
Janel Prator revolutionized banana pudding with
a tasty twist. Using some of the finest
ingredients and an assortment of unique fruits
and cookies, Janel created 40 flavors of delicious
puddings for her loyal customers to enjoy. Her
puddings can be found at The Puddery truck,
local restaurants and delivered to your door.

Puddery

A Puddery is an establishment that produces and sells a variety of unique puddings.

Contact Janel Prator

www.thepuddery.com

info@thepuddery.com

Social Media - @thepuddery

Caren Avedon

Achieving International Notoriety as a Wine & Water Consultant, Miss Avedon is additionally an accomplished Culinary Alchemical Chef & Ormes Collector. Recently becoming a Speaker & Coach regarding Multi-Dimensional Balancing for 21st Century Wellness & Super Natural Awareness, she produces Ancient Proprietary Blends which have become Powerful Sources to Enhance Regenerative Healing, Breath & Meditation.

Quansciousness

The soul awareness at zenith awakening into infinity & the quantum physics of it.

Contact Caren Avedon

Multi Dimensional Balancing Coach, Spontaneous Inspired Speaker & Hermit

WineInMind@netzero.net

Instagram: carenavedon

Facebook: Caren Avedon & Caren Michelle Avedon

Jeri Taylor-Swade

    With no knowledge or understanding of the Direct Sales/Network Marketing/MLM industry, Jeri became a SeneGence distributor in 1999 In 3 yrs. she had achieved the title of Queen (6.5 Million in Team Sales in 1 year) and was the First Queen of SeneGence.

    Jeri is a Master of Beauty and Business, Author, Podcaster, International Trainer, Motivational Speaker and Certified Elite MUA.

Queen

Regal, Classy, Royal, Ruler, Powerful, Commanding, Successful, Not afraid to Fail, Authority, Jeri Taylor-Swade

Contact Jeri Taylor-Swade

www.JeriTaylorSwade.com
www.LiquidMakeup.com
702-524-4490
kissesfromJeri@getlips.com
PodCast: www.CuppawiththeQueen.com
FaceBook: Kisses from Jeri
Instagram: LiquidMakeup_USA
Twitter: kissesfromLV
Linked In: Jeri Taylor-Swade
Tumblr: Jeri Taylor-Swade

Janie Lidey

Janie Lidey's a speaker, bestselling author, Emmy winning songwriter and Grammy winning music educator. Janie speaks and sings at events across the country encouraging her audiences to calm their fear, leap with faith, lean into their purpose and expect blessings and miracles. Janie was recently diagnosed with stage 4 metastatic breast cancer and after being told it was incurable, Janie is cancer free.

Radiate

To emit love with waves powerful enough to create an awakening in human kind.

Contact Janie Lidey

www.janielidey.com

907-227-6410

janie.lidey@gmail.com

Baeth Davis

Baeth Davis is known as the "Palm Pilot for the Soul of Your Business™." With her expertise in scientific hand analysis and human design, she helps you unleash your life purpose, and uncover the #1 thing that has been holding you back from achieving it.

Rant

Radical authenticity. Necessary truth.

Contact Baeth Davis

https://baeth.com

Podcast, "The Rant"
http://Baeth.com/ApplePodcasts.

Email: support@Baeth.com

Karen Daniels

Through workshops, consultations and blogs, Karen Daniels inspires you to transform transitions into turning points. She teaches creative strategies of awareness that will strengthen your connection to imagination and inner wisdom.

Realign

Make a shift or adjustment that body,
mind and spirit know as true and natural.

Contact Karen Daniels

1-403-477-9472

www.windsongexpressivearts.com

Karen@windsongexpressivearts.com

385

Sue Mandell

Sue Mandell is an award-winning speaker, #1 bestselling author, and an Addictive Behavior Specialist. She has been featured on ABC, CBS, NBC, and many cable networks. Sue has spoken to audiences of up to 5,000.

For over 30 years, Sue has helped countless people battle addictive behaviors victoriously. She is a Master Practitioner of NLP, a Master Life and Executive Coach.

Recovery

The process of stopping **ANY** Addictive Behavior and returning to a healthy way of living.

Contact Sue Mandell

951-212-0225

suemandell@bettermesolutions.com

Nancy Sardella

If You Think you Should be Getting More Business From Your Networking Efforts.......
Maybe it's Time To Try WRS! This company has 40 Years of Helping your business do more business!

Referral

What goes around comes around.

Contact Nancy Sardella

818-995-6646

info@wrswrs.com

Margo Lovett

Margo Lovett is the creator and host of Her Business Her Voice Her Conversation, a podcast that instructs, inspires and informs (boomer) women reinventing themselves to become entrepreneurs. A Reinvented woman, Margo's first book, Her Business Her Voice Her Reinvention, is a best seller. Between the show and her books, women realize that successful reinvention is possible & there's help for the challenges.

Reinvention

Bold intentional movement towards an expected end; making a dynamic change in thought, deed.

Contact Margo Lovett

Host of Her Business, Her Voice Her Conversation

http://www.vercayradio.com/her-business---her-voice.html

www.Facebook/MargoGoBeyond.com
http:///www.linkedin.com/in/margolovett/

Office: land line 310 768 1346 (PST)

Ann Bennett

Ann Bennett, the creative genius, of Renegade Branding, a brand profit builder. She helps entrepreneurs build a strong 6-figure business and brand that express's their unique fascination factor and spotlights their talents, skills and abilities. RenegadeBranding.com

Renegade

Someone inspired to disrupt the status quo in order to design an extraordinary life.

Contact Ann Bennett

AnnBennettMarketing.com

Mobile: 646-345-6671

Office: 949-287-6410

annpbennett@gmail.com

Renée Boudreau Salmon

Renée Boudreau Salmon, solo petpreneur and
professional pet sitter, has been pampering pets
for over 18 years as owner of Renée's Concierge
Pet Sitting & Dog Walks. She is licensed,
insured, bonded, Pet CPCR certified, and
member of Pet Sitters International. Every day,
animals, rescues and shelters face life and death
challenges. A portion of profits is donated to
local rescues.

Rescue

trauma, pain, agony, fear, despair, hopelessness, heartbreaking Compassion, Hope, UNconditional Love, infinite Patience, Immeasurable Joy

Contact Renée Boudreau Salmon

310-386-9749

ReneesConcierge4Pets@gmail.com

http://www.LomitaPetSitting.com/

Mary Jadwisiak

Internationally recognized speaker and trainer on hope, recovery & suicide prevention, Mary provides quality, insightful and entertaining workshops based on her advocacy work & personal recovery journey. Mary has delivered keynotes, workshops and continuing education to international corporations, state governments, counties and private agencies throughout the country.   She is committed to hope and is a living example of recovery.

Resilience

The ability to keep going and keep growing.

Contact Mary Jadwisiak

www.holdingthehope.com

360-687-7954

Mary@HoldingTheHope.com

Dr. Hepsharat Amadi, MD

I am a native of New York, who graduated from Bronx H.S. of Science in 1974, Harvard U. in 1979, S.U.N.Y. at Stony Brook Medical School in 1987 and Bronx-Lebanon Hospital Family Practice Residency in 1990. I moved to South Florida in 1990, where I have been in private practice since 2001, doing functional medicine and quantum bio-feedback.

Resonance

The specific frequency at which an object tends to vibrate naturally.

Contact Dr. Hepsharat Amadi, MD

www.dramadi.com

dramadi@dramadi.com

Office phone 954-757-0064

10189 W. Sample Rd.,
Coral Springs, FL 33065

Sarita Wilson

I have been in the workplace in one role or another since the tender age of eleven. At twelve, I wrote my very first résumé. There were only two entries on it, but I was very proud of what I had already accomplished. My desire to write was also realized at that time. Writing has remained a constant in my life.

Resume

Practical, real life experiences in professional and creative work. Execution that's productive, proficient and accomplished.

Contact Sarita Wilson

saritabwilson@outlook.com

504-419-0154

8158 Woodlyn Road
Houston, TX 77028-1950

Tamara Burkett

Tamara has a master's degree in Organizational Management and over 14 years experience developing strategic relationships for international nonprofit organizations. She currently consults business owners helping them keep the customers they attract. ***Tamara does this*** by providing a simple structure and effective strategies in the four customer pillars; service/ support, experience, segmentation, and referrals.

Retention

The action of absorbing and continuing to keep someone or something in your memory.

Contact Tamara Burkett

WWW.TamaraBurkett.com

tamara@tamaraburkett.com

414-803-9689

Craig Duswalt

Craig Duswalt is a Keynote Speaker, Author, Podcaster, and the creator of the brands RockStar Marketing and Rock Your Life. He's a #1 Amazon Best-Selling author, and has written eight books. He toured with Guns N' Roses, as Axl Rose's personal assistant, and Air Supply, as the band's personal assistant.

He features Rock Your Life Weekends every Spring and Fall in Los Angeles.

RockStar

Entrepreneurs who understand that to be successful you MUST market yourself better than everyone else.

Contact Craig Duswalt

www.CraigDuswalt.com

805-241-8170

280 N. Westlake Blvd., Suite 110
Westlake Village, CA 91362

David Kauffman

David Kauffman is a Composer, Screenwriter,
Film Producer, and Founder of Good For The
Soul Music™, San Antonio, TX. Our Mission:
"Song and Story for Healing and Hope on Stage
and Screen."

Sacramenta

The seed planted within that calls me to be and become my best loving self.

Contact David Kauffman

www.goodforthesoulmusic.com

www.davidkauffman.com

www.theoneiwroteforyou.com

www.massofrenewal.com

S

Paul J. Barbe

Paul Barbe is a new author and entrepreneur. He lives in Glendora, California with his wife Gale and has an adult daughter. Paul works a full-time job as a civil engineer. He enjoys sailing and woodworking as hobbies. Please watch for further material from Paul as he explores and sharing his observations of life and world from his unique perspective.

Sail

Tacking and gybing through life using God's gifts. There's no direct course to pursuing happiness.

Contact Paul J. Barbe

626-905-5243

pjbarbe@gmail.com

www.theknauticallife.com

S

Cheryl E. Burget

CEO of Your Sales Genius, Cheryl E. Burget is a fun and highly effective sales expert who helps entrepreneurs and small business owners to increase their sales through authenticity, integrity and service.

Sales

The true meaning of SALES is serving, anyone, lovingly, effectively and successfully.

Contact Cheryl E. Burget

cheryl@yoursalesgenius.com

www.yoursalesgenius.com

303-929-8542

Anthony Camacho

Anthony Camacho, aka "HITMAN" a Multi-Published Best Selling Author, Founder of the Top Producer Factory, international sales performance trainer and motivational speaker.

He has completed over 500 training workshops for companies and entrepreneurs worldwide. A Dale Carnegie Coach and graduate from (iPEC). Learn to write your own paycheck and increase your sales performance.

Salesman

The privilege to sell services to help others solve their problems and enrich their life

Contact Anthony Camacho

www.topproducerfactory.com

hitman@camachocoaching.com

https://youtu.be/n8g0BddDNJc

$\mathcal{S}$

Kelly Pratt

Kelly Pratt, founder of "So, do it! Society" for women who crave connection and ready to make SH!fT happen. Mentor to creative entrepreneurs, she dives deep with to find her clients "creative rhythm" – as they turn their ideas and passions into products, artistic creations, books or fabulous new business ventures.

Salon

A gathering for connection, inspiration and important conversation led by a Salonnière.

Contact Kelly Pratt

Founder & Salonnière
So, do it! Society

http://sodoitsociety.com

http://members.sodoitsociety.com

651-504-4278

hello@sodoitsociety.com

Pamela Levine, M.D.

Dr. Levine specializes in the mind-body connection and works with clients to overcome health obstacles. She has personally experienced and overcome chronic pain and breast cancer. Dr. Levine obtained her medical degree at Duke University and residency certification in Family Medicine at the University of Iowa. She has additional training in acupuncture, integrative medicine, NLP, and hypnotherapy.

Salubrious

Healthy, wholesome, beneficial, favorable. If related to a place may also mean clean or pleasant.

Contact Pamela Levine, M.D.

doitnowcoaching@gmail.com

Shari Sambursky

Shari Sambursky is a Certified Life and Career Coach, specialized in Shadow work. She helps people live their best lives and find a career path that feels aligned.

Samobor

Creative, beauty, joyful, skill, love, light and clarity.

Contact Shari Sambursky

LinkedIn:
https://www.linkedin.com/in/sharisambursky/

Instagram:
https://www.instagram.com/sharisambursky/?hl=en

Join me on Twitter: @sharisambursky

Elyse Rothstein

Elyse Rothstein, a locksmith since 1981
has owned her company since 1984. She
believes in volunteering and supporting her
community. Elyse has been president twice of
the Rotary club and Chamber of Commerce. She
is married to the perfect man, has seven
grandchildren and loves to travel. Elyse has a
storefront location and 5 mobile service vehicles
ready to serve customers.

Security

Comfort, Safety, Protected, Deadbolts,
Peacefulness, Family, Safes, Cozy,
Secure, Relaxed, Alarms, Closeness,
Locked-down, Guarded, Loved-ones

Contact Elyse Rothstein

Industrial Lock and Security, Inc

401 Main Street
El Segundo, CA 90245

P:310-322-3252
F:310-322-3627

www.Industriallock.com
info@industriallock.com

Jan Robinson

Jan Robinson, M.A. is a sex and relationship
mentor, best-selling author, and transformational
speaker. She has helped hundreds of women,
men, and couples have and enjoy deeper, more
fulfilling sex and intimacy. She is the founder of
Multidimensional Pleasure, offering teachings
on the topics of women's sexuality, attracting
your ideal mate, and relationship fulfillment.

Sex

The dynamic interplay between complementary forces driven by a desire to create life.

Contact Jan Robinson

jan@multidimensionalpleasure.com

www.multidimensionalpleasure.com

510-469-8268

Yvonia Payne

Yvonia Payne is the CEO of Savvy Sexy Sheek Fashion a Clothing and Accessories Boutique (www.savvysexysheek.com). She is also a Motivational and Inspirational Speaker who provides present and upcoming entrepreneurs with information on goal setting and information required to start a business. She dedicates her Business Structure and Organizational Discipline to working 20+ years for Corporate America overseeing 100+ clients daily.

Sexy

Sexy is Savvy, Sensuous, Sultry, Seductive, Stylish, Exquisite, Enchanting, Xenodochial, Virtuous, Vivacious, Romantic, Coquettish, Attractive.

Contact Yvonia Payne

www.savvysexysheek.com

www.yvoniapayne.com

PO BOX 970968
Miami, Florida 33197

Phone: 786-701-5958
Toll Free: 1-888-669-1135

Email: ypayne@savvysexysheek.com

Christine Alisa

Christine Alisa, MS is a seasoned alternative therapist and shaman who peels back the layers of the unknown core issues revealing the open person inside who attracts new rich experiences.

Shamanism

Shamanism is an ancient spiritual practice that connects us with our compassionate animal spirit guides.

Contact Christine Alisa

Christine Alisa, MS

chris@christinealisa.com

www.christinealisa.com

S

Denise Thomson

Denise Thomson, Certified Health and Wellness Coach, nurse, fitness trainer, educator, speaker and published bestselling author, has 40 + years of experience in health care. She has saved 2 lives while in College by recognizing the signs of blood poisoning. She consoled people who lost a loved one, and is passionate about helping others living a healthy, balanced life.

Sharing

Sharing is caring; giving; generosity; unselfishness; distribution; a gift; closeness; supporting a family member, friend.

Contact Denise Thomson

Certified Health and Wellness Coach

HC: 896130394

562-335-4956

Coachdenise@ctdigest.net

$\int$

Angel Marie Monachelli

Angel Marie Monachelli is the Creator of the Shine On! Movement™. A National Best-Selling Author of the SHINE ON! book, a highly sought-after Transformational Speaker, Empowerment Coach and Reiki Master. For over 20 years Angel Marie has shown people how to embrace their energy and confidence to create more joy in their lives. Shine On!

Shine

Embracing your unique inner beauty creates energy that radiates a magnificent glow of limitless joy.

Contact Angel Marie Monachelli

Author of SHINE ON!

623-334-3393

http://angelmarieshines.com/

S

Janeth "JayDee" Diaz

68% of non-retired Americans fear running out of money during retirement: What you don't know, WILL hurt you! Learn the 6 steps to Financial Independence at www.FinancialEducation4Free.com. I can help you S.O.A.R. thru good and bad economic times because, it's not how much you make, but how much you keep!

Soar

SURGE, OPTIMIZE, ACQUIRE, RE-CREATE - Ascend thru adversity; rise above the masses; thrive/reach higher level.

Contact Janeth "JayDee" Diaz
License #: 0M35131

Follow me on FB/IG/IN
@JayDeeSolutions

www.Facebook.com/JayDeeSolutions
www.Instagram.com/JayDeeSolutions
www.LinkedIn.com/in/JayDeeSolutions

You may also reach/message me at
www.M.Me/JayDeeSolutions

Katrina Garcia

Katrina Garcia manages one of the most unique web and membership design companies around. With over 30+ years in the corporate sector and 12+ years as a business owner she works to bring forth integrity, honesty, and quality for her clients. Her goal is to help her client's grow their business with exceptional web and membership sites that draws their target audience in.

Social-Safety

Staying socially safe is key in today's business world. So how safe is you're online presence?

Contact Katrina Garcia

www.KGWebsiteDesigns.com

805-402-5957

kgarcia@KGWebsiteDesigns.com

Krista Rose Deane

Krista Rose Deane is a dreamer, and a visionary. She has been passionate about being a part of the Global Shift to a clean green future since 2017.

Krista is helping people transform the way WE think about solar. Her goal is to educate homeowners in the difference between owning vs renting their energy from large corporations.

Solar

Energy, Renewable Recourses, Sunlight, Electricity, Sustainability, Natural Resource, Solar Panels, Environmentalist, Power, Clean Energy, Disruption, Homeowners.

Contact Krista Rose Deane

www.theriseup.ca

250-588-5516

krista@theriseup.ca

$\mathcal{S}$

Jessica Schaffer

Jessica Schaffer is a 2019 Graduate from the University of Tampa with a BA in Applied Dance with a Minor in Sociology. She hopes to go on to be a dance therapist for kids with special needs, mental illness, and fatal disease.

Sonder

Realizing that each passerby is living a life as vivid and complex as your own.

Contact Jessica Schaffer

631-617-4227

jessschaffer97@gmail.com

S

Mary Anne Kurzen

Mary Anne Kurzen is an author, speaker and life coach. She grew up in southern California, has studied, taught and directed travel programs in the United States and abroad. she recently founded ASAP Success and helps individuals and leaders set and realize their goals.

Sparkle

When we show up joyfully, sparking people and places around us. It's catching!

Contact Mary Anne Kurzen

661-877-3353

maryannekurzen@gmail.com

maryanne@globaledtraining.com

Melody Keymer Harper

Melody Keymer Harper, speaker, bestselling author, entertainer, and Radio/TV Host, has shared the stage and screen with celebrities **Elvis Presley**, **Johnny Carson**, **Elizabeth Taylor** and speaking giants: **Brian Tracy**, **Les Brown**, and **Jack Canfield**. Over 40 years experience teaching, speaking and communication skills to stand out as a Celebrity in your industry, get more clients, and make more money.

Speak

Convey your message with authenticity, clarity, and confidence to powerfully impact your audience.

Contact Melody Keymer Harper

www.IgniteYourSpeakingPower.com

melody@IgniteYourSpeakingPower.com

949-400-8111

Marlena E. Uhrik

Author of "The Secret Sauce of Staging,"
Marlena has been staging homes beginning with
her beloved dollhouse as a child! She became an
educator, with a Doctorate degree, and loved
staging homes for friends and family. Marlena
learned interior design, Feng Shui, and became a
Certified Home Stager. She has professionally
staged homes in Sacramento for the last 10
years.

Staging

Showcasing a home's best features, creating an emotional connection, for the greatest number of buyers.

Contact Marlena E. Uhrik

Amazing-Staging.com

916-800-3295

Marlena@Amazing-Staging.com

S

Arlene Santos, MBA, MHCM, RN

My great passion is to help you get to where you want to go, be who you want to be, and have what you want to have. Sometimes, we are our own worst enemies and I help my clients get unstuck as they strive toward success and abundance.

Stand

To maintain an upright position, rooted and grounded to withhold life's fiercest storms.

Contact Arlene Santos

Certified John Maxwell Coach

623-337-0804

Arlene.Esse@gmail.com

www.personaldevelopmentaz.com

Ranchelle Van Bryce

Ranchelle, founder of Stiletto Enterprises Inc. is an Intuitive Business Strategist. She uses Science, Technology and Love to help create the business of your dreams, without the agony of facing burnout and losing out on family time.

She shares with her clients a formula that she has used over and over again to create a business that is fun and financially successful.

Stiletto

Brilliant, powerful, authentic, and vulnerable. Standing in femininity with no apologies. Radiating love for self.

Contact Rancelle Van Bryce

780-679-7275

Ranchelle@StilettoEnterprisesInc.com

S

Richard A. McCullough

Richard McCullough wrote his first short story at age 10 and hasn't stopped since. He has 11 published books and has just finished a three-volume historical saga. He is the creator of Story Tech, the ancient technology of storytelling codified and de-mystified. While being a philosopher at heart, he spends most of his time teaching fiction writing through books, lectures and videos.

Story

How a culture defines itself, where it's been, where it is and where it's going.

Contact Richard A. McCullough

626-644-7025

www.Write-Better-Fiction.com

rich.writer@gmail.com

S

Joyce Khoury

Business Philosophy and Mission:

My mission is to help people from all walks of life understand their medical insurance options by acting as a mentor and educator. I hold myself to the highest level of personal and professional integrity and promise only to offer services and solutions that improve their wellbeing.

Strong

Provides The Basis For Integrity, Intelligence And Most Importantly Love Of Our Fellow Human Beings.

Contact Joyce Khoury

Medicare Coach 101

www.joyce@medicarecoach101.com
https://medicarecoach101.com

joyce@medicarecoach101.com

8405 Pershing Drive, #301
Playa del Rey, CA 90293

Tel.: 310-383-6452

Fax: 310-821-7300

$\int$

Reinhard Kurzen

Reinhard Kurzen MS has 20 years of Healthy Building Consulting in 50 countries. He has 44 years Practice/Teaching TM. Being a Catalyst in raising Consciousness.

Surrender

To Let SPIRIT Run my Life.

Contact Reinhard Kurzen

818-421-6319

Reinhardvonwewel@gmail.com

𝒮

Randy Peyser

Randy Peyser is a Book Editor and Ghostwriter, who pitches manuscripts to publishers. Her authors are featured in: Oprah Magazine, Time Magazine, the Wall Street Journal and USA Today Bestseller Lists, Hallmark TV, and airport bookstores. Randy is the author of: The Write-a-Book Program; Crappy to Happy in the movie, "Eat Pray Love"; and The Power of Miracle Thinking.www.AuthorOneStop.com

Synchro-butt-nicity

When you accidentally butt dial someone but the timing was absolutely perfect that you did so!

Contact Randy Peyser

AUTHOR ONE STOP, INC.
Randy Peyser, CEO

831-726-3153

www.AuthorOneStop.com

S

Nika Roback

With a broad experience spanning over 17 years, Nika Roback creates personalized spaces that bring to life an artistic vision while preserving functionality suited to various lifestyles of her clients.

She believes your surroundings have a direct impact on other areas of your life so she coined the phrase: Enhance your home, enhance your life.

Synergize

It is teamwork, open-mindedness, and the adventure of finding new solutions to old problems.

Contact Nika Roback

UNIK interior designs

www.UNIKinteriordesigns.com

805-864-2585

$\mathcal{S}$

459

Dora Herrera

The Herrera Family prepares food the old-fashioned way ~ our family recipes are cooked daily in small batches, using only the freshest ingredients. In the more than 4 decades since we opened Yuca's Hut, thousands of awards, articles, and reviews let us know that we're cooking what you love!

Taco

Little bite. Teaser. Delicious. Craving. Snack. Mexican sounds good right now. Meet you at Yuca's!

Contact Yuca's Restaurants
Socorro, Margarita and Dora Herrera

www.yucasla.com

626-788-7448

kitchen@yucasla.com

FB: Yuca's Restaurants

Instagram, Twitter: @yucasla

Lynne M. Price

With over 30 years of tax, accounting and business consulting experience, I have always enjoyed counseling individuals and business owners to achieve financial independence. I have been a CFO and business advisor for multiple companies, and I have assisted many clients in navigating through our complex tax system enabling them to minimize their personal tax burden.

Tax

A monetary levy on citizens to operate and main government services.

Contact Lynne M. Price, CPA

taxedgepro.com

lynne@lynnepricecpa.com

Judy Yates

Judy Yates has been a practicing public accountant focused on matters of taxation for 30 years. While she's been working primarily from the Chicago area, she's always served her clients wherever they have roamed both within and outside of the United States. "Knowing the rules of taxation makes it possible to minimize the negative impact they have on the pocketbook, saving clients real money."

Taxation

A system of involuntary levies imposed, usually by government, on its citizen / members.

Contact Judy Yates, CPA

JYatesCPA@gmail.com

Office: 773-465-5245

Cell: 773-506-2727

Deborah Morgan

Debbie Morgan, CPA is the founder of Deborah Morgan and Company Inc., a full-service tax and accounting firm. Her company caters to entrepreneurs, individuals, as well as non-profits. Debbie is passionate about educating new business owners and helping them overcome their tax and accounting fears so they may focus on their passion – growing their business.

Taxes

Money assessed by the Government to function. A tax professional will help you save money.

Contact Deborah Morgan, CPA

805-496-2828

www.DeborahMorganAndCompany.com

Suzy Prudden

Internationally acclaimed speaker and seminar leader, author, fitness expert, master hypnotherapist, body/mind pioneer, success and mindset coach and book publisher. You've seen her on Oprah, The Today Show and Good Morning America. The New York Times says, "If Suzy is talking about it today, the rest of the country will be talking about it tomorrow."

Temerity

An over abundance of self-confidence.

Contact Suzy Prudden

310-640-8885

suzyprudden@gmail.com

ittybittypublishing.com

suzyprudden.com

311 Main St., Suite D
El Segundo, CA 90245

T

Heather Hockney

Heather Hockney resides in Phoenix, AZ with the love of her life and their 4 fur-babies. When she isn't assisting others in the pursuit of their dream home, she's either camping, hunting, or PC gaming with friends; or enjoying a crisp beer while watching a Netflix original with her love & best friend, Abraham.

Tenacious

Not readily relinquishing a position, principle, or course of action; determined; persistent.

Contact Heather Hockney

480-822-8284

HockneyAZHomes@gmail.com

Lisa Thomas

Lisa Thomas empowers individuals to reach their full potential by removing inherited emotional blocks, such as overwhelm, abandonment, procrastination and scarcity. Her expertise in removing negative energy and inherited patterns empowers people to get their gifts and talents out into the world, confidently and in alignment with their Soul's purpose.

Transformation

Let go of your past; Live in the present; Trust your future holds good things.

Contact Lisa Thomas

lisa@lisathomasenergyhealing.com

http://lisathomasenergyhealing.com

Lisa Browne McCulloch

Lisa Browne McCulloch is a Hypnotherapist, Energy Healer, and Spiritual Coach in the Costa Mesa, Orange County area. She specializes in hypnosis, energy clearing and healing spaces. She is certifying as a Positive Prime provider. In addition, Lisa is an account executive at BGR and a board member of the Inside Edge.

Transmutation

Something or someone is elevated it to a higher state.

Contact Lisa Browne McCulloch, CHt, CHi, MA

yourheartandsoulmusic@gmail.com

Shantha Mony

Luxury Destinations Concierge is passionate about curating custom experiences for our clients to all corners of the world. We work with local experts to craft unique itineraries for individuals, families as well as arrange group travel. Our core mission is to provide our clients with memorable vacation packages that are directly in line with their personal tastes, desires and pocketbook.

Travel

Travel Expanding your mind to different cultures by visiting places beyond your familiar surroundings.

Contact Shantha Mony

Luxury Destinations Concierge

www.luxurydestinationsconcierge.com

805-236-4437

Tamiza Teja

Tamiza is artisan, chef, and owner of Tamiza's Treats featuring artisan treats and foodie-themed gifts. Tamiza is a baker and treat maker offering a variety of cakes, cookies, fudge, popcorn, and more delicious yummy things, as well as designer and maker of fun foodie-themed selections of beautiful handmade beaded jewelry, greeting cards, keychains, and other fun essentials. Seize the day, have dessert first!

Treat

Anything that creates happiness. A treat is great for gift giving or self-celebration.

Contact Tamiza Teja
Artisan/Chef/Owner

Tamiza's Treats

tamiza@tamizastreats.com

http://www.tamizastreats.com/
https://www.facebook.com/TamizasTreats
https://twitter.com/TamizasTreats
https://instagram.com/tamizastreats/

Karen DeSantis-Meyer

My name is Karen DeSantis Meyer.
I trust my authentic self and strive to bring value
and truth to people in helping them discover
their "sleeping giant" within. It is an honor to be
part of someone's personal growth journey and
watch them emerge into their God given talents.

I TRUST in HIM daily.

Trust

To rely on unshakeable strength. A place of firm confidence and belief in someone or something.

Contact Karen DeSantis-Meyer

Karendesantis.nerium.com

karendesantis@sbcglobal.net

818-438-9409

Angelia D. McGowan

Angelia D. McGowan, author of Celebrate!
CARs, Women and the Road Less Traveled,
provides public relations and writing services to
entrepreneurs and small businesses through her
Colorado-based company, Canady's Corner,
LLC.

Ubuntu

We're all in this together; this roller-coaster ride called life

Contact Angelia D. McGowan

www.canadyscorner.com

U

Deborah Kagan

Deborah Kagan is a Speaker, Author and Mentor with years of practice being a turned-on woman. For over 25 years, she's helped women tap into their innate power and connect with their Mojo, which is the source of true self-esteem. Join her in the UNDRESSED conversation on Instagram (@therealundressed) and subscribe to the podcast on iTunes.

Undressed

Stripped down to the bare essence. No filter, fluff or walls. Vulnerable truth. Self-love.

Contact Deborah Kagan

www.TheRealUndressed.com

yes@therealundressed.com

855-900-6656

$\mathcal{U}$

Wieslaw "Wes" Rocki, M.D., Ph.D.

Wes Rocki M.D., Ph.D. offers an unorthodox
perception of self-healing as the core aspect of
health and life. He dedicated 40 years of medical
practice, research, and spiritual explorations to
studying, practicing and teaching self-healing
care. Dr. Rocki inspires patients to explore and
heal the essential, yet unorthodox root causes of
their diseases, for example, the memories of
traumatic childhood.

Unorthodox

Free from the imposed limitations.
Example: unorthodox medicine inspires
patients to practice self-healing care.

Contact
Wieslaw "Wes" Rocki, M.D., Ph.D.

www.selfhealingcare.com

https://www.facebook.com/selfhealingcar
e/

https://www.linkedin.com/in/wesrockimd
phd/

(202) 615 8377

drwesr@gmail.com

Christine Lapidus

My clients build financial balance, protecting their families, and businesses from the many threats to their financial wellbeing. I help teach them to protect, save, invest and grow their resources so that they can have – "A Good Life, For the Rest of Your Life."

Unselfie

A financial plan to benefit family, friends or charities in the most tax efficient manner.

Contact Christine Lapidus

christine_lapidus@pacificadvisors.com

818-920-8395

www.pacificadvisors.com/clapidus

Maureen A. Pisani

Originally from the Island of Malta, Maureen's a
Motivational Speaker, Author, Hypnotherapist.
She co-authored a paper through the Neuro-
Science Department at UCLA. She's authored
10 books and 25 CDs. She's at the Masters
Level in Hypnotherapy, Therapeutic Guided
Imagery, Neuro-Linguistic Programming and
Reiki Energy; and teaches the first three. She's
also the Resident Therapist at the Chopra Center
in San Diego, California.

Unstoppable

Determined continuous motion that overcomes every, any & all obstacles to achievement of undeniable success.

Contact Maureen A. Pisani

www.prothrivesbh.com

619-252-2253

maureen.pisani@yahoo.com

LinkedIn - https://www.linkedin.com/in/maureenpisanihypnotherapy/

FB - https://www.facebook.com/prothrivesciencebasedhypnotherapy/

Candace Webb-Henderson

Born a twin in Danville, Illinois, Candace Webb-Henderson followed in the same footsteps as her beloved mother, Joan Doyle Webb, and her grandmother, Dorothy Burr Doyle, working in the medical industry helping others. Her greatest inspiration was her mom signing the words in the palm of her hand on her deathbed. She told Candace to finish the book, *Blessed to Be Unwanted.*

.Unwanted

An extraordinary testament to how one woman's love transformed an *unwanted* baby into a triumph!

Contact Candace Webb-Henderson

https://candacewebbhenderson. com

949-584-7618

candy@candacewebbhenderson.com

henderson6262@yahoo.com

U

Nancy Urbach

I am embarking on a search of self-discovery. I desire to seek and identify people, places, and things that make me feel good and that are a great vibrational match. Come, join me on my journey, and find out how to discover your own vibrational and energetic matches.

Vibration

I am vibrating energetically in a space where my life feels easy, fulfilled, and amazing!

Contact Nancy Urbach

www.nancybu.com

623-826-5941

contact@nancybu.com

B. A. Victor

Call me Bella Victor, surviving cancer, job loss, erratic behavior in my then spouse (he is a sociopath), then loss of a parent, home, divorce, pets, etc. Let's say I have an appreciation for life and know how to go beyond hurt past surviving to thriving and want to guide others to realize their own gifts and live victoriously!

Victor

Champion, over-comer, winner, beacon, resilient, confident, contributor, pathfinder, authentic, inspiring, gracious, reliable, favored, thriving, fulfilled.

Contact B. A. Victor

Author

www.BAVictor.com

beavictornow@gmail.com

Nettie Owens

Nettie Owens, CPO-CD®, helps businesses get more DONE. She works with entrepreneurs, professionals, and corporations to reach their biggest goals through accountability and productivity. *Nettie is a nationally recognized organizing, accountability, and productivity expert.* Her methodologies are brain-based and backed by science. It is her mission to help others to clear the path to their potential.

Vision

A look into the future to create your reality today.

Contact Nettie Owens

momentumaccountability.com

443-904-5412

info@momentumaccountability.com

Stacey Stuart

Stacey Stuart is the owner of Pacific NW Home Staging and the creator of 6S-Toolbox™ Business System, Remodeled Agent & Entrepreneur Coaching Program. Stacey is passionate about helping real estate agents and entrepreneurs with kick-starting and elevating their business to the next level.

Vivacious

A person who is exciting, lively, full of animation, high spirits and tenacity for life.

Contact Stacey Stuart

Stacey Stuart Global

6S-Toolbox™ for Entrepreneurs & Real Estate Professionals

www.StaceyStuartGlobal.com

Stacey@StaceyStuartGlobal.com

Cary MacArthur

Cary MacArthur is a coach, speaker, author, teacher, and student (BA in psychology & Spanish, currently working toward becoming an MFT).

Cary's passionate about connecting to her authenticity, power, and purpose, and helping others do the same.

She and her husband, Dave, have been married 29 years. They have five kids and six grandkids. Grandma ("Rassy") is her favorite title.

Voice

An authentic connection to one's purpose
and Value through Openness, Intentional
action, Clearing, & Expression

Contact Cary MacArthur

CaryMacArthur.com

435-313-3870

carymacarthur@gmail.com

Facebook: Cary Mac Arthur
Instagram: @carymac
twitter: @carymac

Janet Kunst

Janet Kunst is the owner and founder of Recipes for Marketing Success. With over 25 years of marketing experience, Janet's passion is for small businesses that struggle with their online marketing. From social media and blogging to podcasting and everything in between, Janet helps you discover your unique Recipe for Marketing Success that will make your business sizzle!

Voluntold

When someone in authority tells you that they volunteered you to perform a task.

Contact Janet Kunst

Founder & Chief Social Media Officer

janet@RecipesforMarketingSuccess.com

https://RecipesforMarketingSuccess.com

949-861-0820

Debbie Sholk

Debbie Sholk has been an educator, corporate trainer, entrepreneur, editor, dachshund wrangler, and weaver of stories for the past 30 years. She is an astute observer of human behavior and has lived in 4 countries, most recently, the Republic of Texas. Her coaching skills are highly sought after by those who know her.

Wanderlust

Pleasure in exploring. Stepping out; being a pioneer in a realm that feeds your soul.

Contact Debbie Sholk

469-626-7882

sharpcookieintx@gmail.com

JJ Lee

JJ Lee is an actor with voiceover credits in television, film and online, and breadth of life experience from Hotshot Forest Firefighter to **Hedge Fund Leader**, Satellite Engineer and Program Manager, to Entrepreneur and Naval Officer serving as Acting Battle Force Commander and Commodore of a Destroyer Squadron, Acting Regional Commander of US Forces in Afghanistan, and five years on a SEAL Team.

Water

The most important compound on the planet. We're mostly made of it.
Drink the best!

Contact JJ Lee

www.Kangenator.com

www.JJLeeVoice.com

Rennie Gabriel

Rennie Gabriel went from broke at age 50 to multi-millionaire in just a few years. He now shows others how to do the same through his books, online programs and coaching and donates all his profits to the charity www.ShelterToSoldier.org. Rennie is available to do podcast and media interviews and speak to government groups, corporations and associations.

Wealth

When the amount of money from your income producing assets exceeds your lifestyle requirements.

Contact Rennie Gabriel

www.WealthOnAnyIncome.com

818-298-7555

rennie@WealthOnAnyIncome.com

Lupe Silva

Lupe Silva, a Certified Wellness Coach used "Food as Medicine" to transform herself from sick & tired to healthy & happy. After 20+ yrs in Corporate HR, she left to create & teach The Wow! Program which helps others transform too by incorporating a holistic lifestyle. Ms. Silva resides in Orange County with her husband of 35 years. If not now, When?

Wellness

Wellness is a Healthy Balance of our most precious assets: Mind, Body & Spirit.

Contact Lupe Silva, Wellness Coach

www.WellnessPath.us

714-473-6762

Lupe@WellnessPath.us

Dorine Kramer, MD

As an empty-nester, Dr. Dorine is passionate about helping midlife women who have lost their identity and purpose because of a major life transition like empty-nest. She is a retired MD, now a life coach, energy worker, bestselling author and speaker, helping women to fall in love with themselves and their new lives.

Whimsical

Playfully quaint or fanciful, especially in an appealing or amusing way; unpredictable; freakish.

Contact Dr. Dorine Kramer

Webpage: yourtimetosoar.com

Telephone: 866-653 7377

email: dorine@drdorinekramer.com

515

Diane A. Curran

Diane A. Curran, The Wow Whisperer, is a branding and marketing expert and speaker with a keen creative perspective on the good, the ugly and the extraordinary in modern media. Long steeped in the arts, Diane is equally passionate about marketing as high performance communication. Author of the biz book trilogy **The Marketing Deck**, she hosts the podcast **Wow Whispering**.

Whispering

Using a soft, confidential tone of voice to hint at or deliver a private message.

Contact Diane A. Curran

www.TheMarketingDeal.com

Facebook: https://www.facebook.com/TheMarketing Deal/

Twitter: @wowdianeacurran

Podcast: www.WowWhispering.com

$\mathcal{W}$

Dee Ajayi

Dee has been a business growth specialist for well over the past 31 years. She has helped her clients improve their business practices and increase their revenue by 51% in record time. Her focus today is on water quality and health improvement for homeowners. Her passions are to end religious persecution and stop human trafficking globally.

Wholesome

Something beneficial that enhances life. Conducive to or suggestive of good health and physical well-being.

Contact Dee Ajayi

www.Wholesomebydee.com

817-677-9110

wholesometx@gmail.com

Katrina Wagner

I am a full-time professor of Studio Art, Art
History of the Americas and Ancient
Architecture History at the College of Marin. I
am also a working artist doing realistic acrylic
and oil paintings and both figurative and
abstracted ceramics.

Wild

A wondrous winging away from the norm,
WILD frees us all to create our path.

Contact Katrina Wagner

www.katrinawagner.com

415-699-3231

katrinawagner@yahoo.com

Sherry Winn

Sherry Winn is a leader of leaders and a visionary of visionaries, founder and CEO of The Winning Leadership Company. Her company guarantees: 1) Leaders That Inspire; 2) Teams That Deliver, and 3) Cultures That Win!

Win

The ability to unleash the potential within you allowing all possibilities of greatness to emerge.

Contact Sherry Win

TheWinningLeadershipcompany.com

sherry@TheWinningLeadershipCompany.com

304-380-4398

Stephen Charles Carpenter

BLESSED SACRED™ represents the inevitable awakening of human consciousness upon mother earth and our realization as divine infinite spiritual beings. Earth school comprises a transformational healing opportunity for each of us, family. Do the work. Forgiveness, gratitude, and love are the keys. As Rumi teaches, "You are not a drop in the ocean. You are the entire ocean in a drop."

Wisdom

"You must be the change you wish to see in the world."

~ Mohandas Karamchand Gandhi

Contact Stephen Charles Carpenter

www.BlessedSacred.com

415-513-8025

BlessedSacred@Protonmail.com

Jill Safran

Like most of you, I'm a carbon life form competing for survival resources on this chaotic planet. However, as a Mindfulness Practitioner, I'm convinced we could minimize our planetary distress with a bit of mindfulness, some compassion for others, and plenty of dark chocolate.

Wise-Mind

An aspect of mindfulness in which reason and emotion align to produce true wisdom.

Contact Jill Safran

Website: http://www.wittymystic.com

Twitter: Jill Safran @WittyMystic

Email: jillsafran@gmail.com

Diane A. Curran

Diane A. Curran, The Wow Whisperer, is a branding and marketing expert and speaker with a keen creative perspective on the good, the ugly and the extraordinary in modern media. Long steeped in the arts, Diane is equally passionate about marketing as high performance communication. Author of the biz book trilogy **The Marketing Deck**, she hosts the podcast **Wow Whispering**.

Wow

An intuitive, instinctive expression voiced in awe, pleasure, or stun when presented with the unexpected.

Contact Diane A. Curran

www.TheMarketingDeal.com

Facebook: https://www.facebook.com/TheMarketingDeal/

Twitter: @wowdianeacurran

Podcast: www.WowWhispering.com

Suzy Prudden

Internationally acclaimed speaker and seminar leader, author, fitness expert, master hypnotherapist, body/mind pioneer, success and mindset coach and book publisher. You've seen her on Oprah, The Today Show and Good Morning America. The New York Times says, "If Suzy is talking about it today, the rest of the country will be talking about it tomorrow."

X-Cellent!

The way you want to feel when you wake up each morning.

Contact Suzy Prudden

310-640-8885

suzyprudden@gmail.com

ittybittypublishing.com

suzyprudden.com

311 Main St., Suite D
El Segundo, CA 90245

Cathy Alessandra

Cathy Alessandra is a business and life coach, aka the YES I CAN Coach. She specializes in integrating your professional life with your personal life while mitigating regrets in both. No woulda, coulda, shouldas here. Cathy uses her 5 step YES method to empower her clients to embrace their fears and refocus their time, energy and efforts for more positive, productive results.

Yes

When used correctly, you experience strength, success, self-care, spirit, sparkle and a sense of self.

Contact Cathy Alessandra

www.CathyAlessandra.com

310-283-5271

cathy@cathyalessandra.com

y

Zeahlot Lopez, LMFT LPCC

Zeahlot Lopez is a Licensed Marriage and Family Therapist, Licensed Professional Clinical Counselor, and Licensed Cosmetologist helping humans rebuild their spirit. Guided by her intuition, clinical training, and life experiences, she currently helps individuals and families lead a happier life! She additionally enjoys providing coaching services to entrepreneurs and those looking to increase their emotional intelligence.

Zeahlot

As unique as her name, Zeahlot, cannot be described for she is beautifully her own.

Contact Zeahlot Lopez, LMFT LPCC
CEO and Founder of Vida Therapy, Inc.

Website: www.VidaTherapy.co

Phone: 310-779-9030

Email: info@VidaTherapy.co

Christina Ammerman

Helping you merge the spiritual into the physical is Christina Ammerman's life purpose. Her healing work focuses on clearing the deepest subconscious patterns that formed your ego, so that you can align with your Higher Self at all times. Discover your deepest patterns by taking the quiz at CoreWoundQuiz.com.

Zenquility™

A state of balance and peace achieved by integrating Spirit into practical everyday matters.

Contact Christina Ammerman

Website: zenquility.com

or follow us on Facebook or Instagram: @zenquility

Misty Zdanski

Misty is a Life Coach & Wellness Advocate with doTERRA. Her passion is to help women connect with their inner truth and help them manifest their heart's desires through mind-body connection, mindfulness practices, and essential oils.

Zest

When an idea pops in your head, do it whole-heartedly with faith; Live with Zest!

Contact Misty Zdanski, MA

Life Coach & doTERRA Wellness Advocate

my.doterra.com/MistyZdanski

www.facebook.com/LoveLifeOils

MistyZdanski@gmail.com

Cynthia Velderrain

Cynthia Velderrain is and has always been an animal lover. Her family was always wondering what kind of animal she would bring home next. Cynthia has since put her love for animals into her life's work as a professional pet trainer, dog walker and pet sitter. She graduated from the Animal Behavior College and is certified in both Pet CPR and First Aid.

Zinger

There was a surprising turn of events at the dog show, the spectators were awed!

Contact Cynthia Velderrain

ccvelderrain@hotmail.com

714-317-6595

Author Index

Author Index

Author Index

Author Index

Author Index

You've finished. Before you go...

Tweet/share that you finished this book.

Please star rate this book

Reviews are solid gold to writers. Please take a few minutes to give us some itty bitty feedback on this book.

*If you enjoyed this Itty Bitty® book
you might also like:*

- <u>Your Amazing Itty Bitty® Business Experts
Compilation Book</u>

Coming Soon!

- Your Amazing Itty Bitty® Health and Wellness
Experts Compilation Book

- Your Amazing Itty Bitty® Coaching Experts
Compilation Book

Made in the USA
Coppell, TX
25 February 2022

74073579R00312